INTERNATIONAL SOCIALISM

A quarterly journal of socialist theory

Autumn 1998
Contents

Editorial

Clare Fermont	*Indonesia: the inferno of revolution*	3
Workers' representatives and socialists	*Three interviews from Indonesia*	35
Chris Bambery	*Report from Indonesia*	45
Tony Cliff	*Revolution and counter-revolution: lessons for Indonesia*	53
John Molyneux	*The legitimacy of modern art*	71
Gary McFarlane	*A respectable trade? Slavery and the rise of capitalism*	103
Paul McGarr	*The French Revolution: Marxism versus revisionism*	113
Shaun Doherty	*Will the real James Connolly please stand up?*	127

Issue 80 of INTERNATIONAL SOCIALISM, quarterly
journal of the Socialist Workers Party (Britain)

Published September 1998
Copyright © International Socialism
Distribution/subscriptions: International Socialism,
PO Box 82, London E3.
American distribution: B de Boer, 113 East Center St, Nutley,
New Jersey 07110.
Subscriptions and back copies: PO Box 16085, Chicago
Illinois 60616
Editorial and production: 0171-538 1626
Sales and subscriptions: 0171-538 5821
American sales: 773 665 7337

ISBN I 898876 40 1

Printed by BPC Wheatons Ltd, Exeter, England
Typeset by East End Offset, London E3
Cover by Sherborne Design Ltd

For details of back copies see the end pages of this book

Subscription rates for one year (four issues) are:

Britain and overseas (surface):	individual	£14.00 ($30)
	institutional	£25.00
Air speeded supplement:	North America	£3.00
	Europe/South America	£3.00
	elsewhere	£4.00

Note to contributors
The deadline for articles intended for issue 81 of
International Socialism is 1 November 1998

All contributions should be double-spaced with wide margins.
Please submit two copies. If you write your contribution
using a computer, please also supply a disk, together with
details of the computer and programme used.

INTERNATIONAL SOCIALISM ★

A quarterly journal of socialist theory

THE REVOLUTION in Indonesia has shaken the ruling class to its foundations. In one of the first full length accounts in English of the crisis in Indonesia Clare Fermont looks at the economic and social background to the revolution and goes on to piece together a compelling narrative of the struggles which toppled Suharto's dictatorship. Our coverage continues by interviewing Indonesian trade union activists and socialists about their experience during the revolution and their assessment of the tasks which now confront the movement. Chris Bambery's 'Report from Indonesia' gives a first hand account of the depth of the continuing crisis and an assessment of the stability of President Habibie's new government. Tony Cliff concludes our Indonesian coverage with an open letter to Indonesian socialists in which he draws on the Marxist tradition to suggest the best strategy for building a revolutionary organisation in Indonesia.

JOHN MOLYNEUX develops the themes of his review of the Royal Academy's 'Sensation' exhibition, published in our last issue, *International Socialism* 79, to provide a general theoretical defence of modern art.

BOOK REVIEWS in this issue include Paul McGarr's overview of debates on the French Revolution, Shaun Doherty taking issue with a new introduction to the writings of the great Irish revolutionary James Connolly, and Gary McFarlane comparing Robin Blackburn's and Hugh Thomas' recent accounts of slavery.

Editor: John Rees. Assistant editors: Alex Callinicos, Chris Harman, John Molyneux, Lindsey German, Colin Sparks, Mike Gonzalez, Peter Morgan, Mike Haynes, Judy Cox, Megan Trudell, Mark O'Brien and Rob Hoveman.

Indonesia: the inferno of revolution

CLARE FERMONT

The story of what has happened in Indonesia is the best possible answer to all those who write off Marxism as irrelevant to the modern world. Such people say that the working class is disappearing. In Indonesia, in just 30 years, the working class grew from less than 10 million to 86 million—far more than the entire world working class at the time Marx and Engels wrote *The Communist Manifesto*. Such people said that the so-called miracle Tiger economies were immune to the traditional booms and slumps of capitalism. In Indonesia the economic slump was more unexpected and catastrophic than Marx himself could have imagined. Such people have been saying that the events of May 1968 in France were a blip on the liberal historical process and will never happen again. In Indonesia, a country four times more populous than France, students have led a mass revolt that is every bit as shattering as that of 30 years ago. In 1968 the revolt spread across Europe and further afield. Today the dictators and governments in Malaysia, Thailand, South Korea and elsewhere are trembling in fear.

Those who write off Marx say that the only way to achieve reforms is to elect educated liberals to parliament and wait for improvements to be handed down. In Indonesia all the evidence of the past few months shows that such liberals are both unwilling and incapable of delivering reforms, and that only when the masses take to the streets do reforms become possible. Those who write off Marx also say that the independent organisation of the most class conscious elements of the working class is not needed under liberal democracy. In Indonesia liberal democrats have stirred up racism, courted favour with international capitalism and stuck their noses into the trough of corruption and greed. Only the organised working class has an interest in fighting racism and the system that is based on profit, not need, and only the organised and politically conscious working class can challenge for state power and seize what is rightfully theirs—the wealth they have produced.

'Indonesia is rich in raw materials yet the people live in misery. The people can no longer afford to eat or buy medicine. This is all the fault of the system—this is what we have to smash.' These words were spoken by student leader Cecep Daryus at a rally shortly before President Thojib Suharto was toppled on 21 May 1998. A few months earlier, the young man would probably never have thought of such words, let alone dared to say them out loud. What was amazing about the overthrow of Suharto, as so often with the fall of dictators, was the speed with which it happened. The anger which exploded to overthrow the dictator who had ruled his people without mercy for 32 years had in fact been building up for some time. This article first looks at the mounting economic crisis facing the old regime and the growing resistance to the dictatorship since the virtual annihilation of opposition in 1965. Secondly, it describes how the uprising unfolded and analyses the main forces of opposition. Thirdly, it outlines the enormous obstacles facing the new government as it tries to grapple with deepening economic crisis and an awakened people, and sets out what steps need to be taken by organised labour and the left to ensure that the revolutionary period Indonesia has entered is pushed forward and the suffering of the masses finally ended.

Suharto: the West's best friend

President Suharto came to power following a military coup in 1965 carried through with such relentless violence that between half a million and a million Indonesians were wiped out within a year. For 32 years, from the moment he butchered his way to power until a few weeks before his overthrow, he was the darling of the West. He offered loyal support against the 'red peril' in the region, a huge market for arms sales, and a massive source of profits from the exploitation of the country's vast natural resources and huge pool of cheap labour.

Suharto was not so popular at home. His rule over the world's fourth most populous country (200 million people) was maintained by brutal repression. All opposition political activity was banned. Peaceful protesters, trade union activists, all those who tried to organise independently were routinely imprisoned, tortured and sometimes assassinated. When Portuguese colonial rule collapsed in East Timor in 1975,

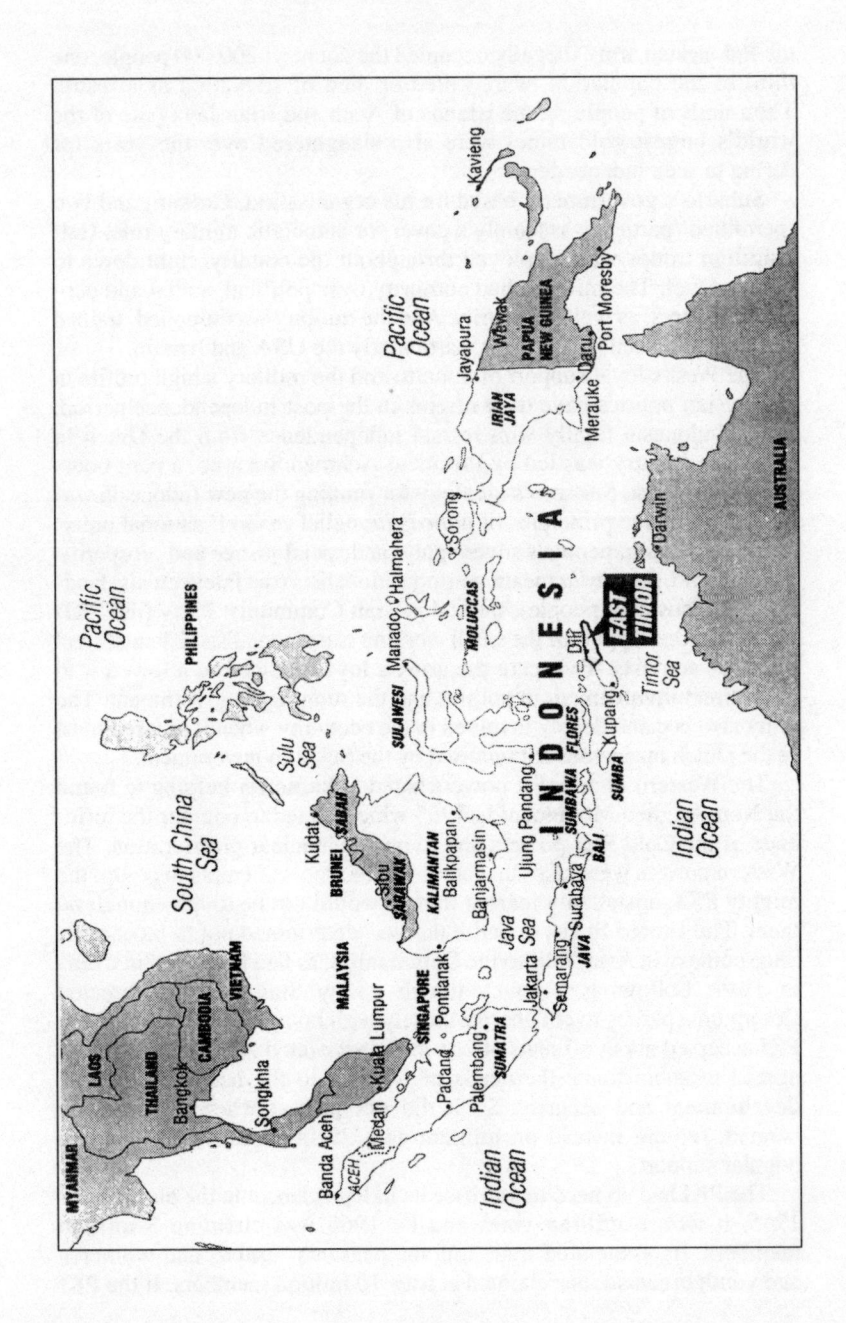

INDONESIA: THE INFERNO OF REVOLUTION

the Indonesian army illegally occupied the country: 200,000 people, one third of the population, were killed or died of starvation as a result. Thousands of people on the islands of Aceh and Irian Jaya (site of the world's largest gold mine) were also slaughtered over the years for daring to seek independence.

Suharto's government, based on his organisation, Golkar[1], and two 'permitted' parties, was simply a cover for autocratic military rule. Half a million troops were deployed throughout the country, right down to village level. The military had authority over political, social and economic matters, as well as security. And the military was supplied, trained and even financed by the West, particularly the USA and Britain.

The West's loyal support of Suharto and the military's high profile in Indonesian politics have their origins in the post-independence period. When Indonesia finally won formal independence from the Dutch in 1949, the country was led by President Achmed Sukarno, a petit bourgeois nationalist. Sukarno's ideology for running the new Indonesia was based on the five principles of *pancasila*: belief in God; national unity; humanitarianism; people's sovereignty; and social justice and prosperity. For Sukarno, *pancasila* meant uniting nationalists (the intellectuals, landlords and business people); the Indonesian Communist Party (the PKI) which had the support of the small working class; socialists; Islamists and religious activists. To secure the army's loyalty, Sukarno allowed it to have direct involvement in politics and the running of government. The army also became deeply involved in the economy when it secured most of the Dutch businesses nationalised by the Sukarno government.

The Western imperialist powers hated Sukarno for helping to found the Non-Aligned Movement in 1955 which aimed to counter the influence of the Cold War powers and to oppose nuclear proliferation. The Western powers were also suspicious of Sukarno's attempts to co-opt the mighty PKI, mistakenly fearing that he would not be tough enough on them. The United States in particular was determined not to let another huge country in Asia 'fall' to the Communists, as had happened in China in 1949. Following a policy drawn up by Stalin, which directed Communist parties to collaborate closely with bourgeios nationalists, the PKI accepted about 60 seats of 261 in the appointed Assembly. The PKI agreed to subordinate the needs of workers to the needs of national development and security. So it did not protest when strikes were banned, relying instead on militant anti-US imperialism to maintain popular support.

The PKI had no need to sacrifice its independence. In the elections of 1955, it won 6 million votes and by 1965 was claiming 3 million members. Its associated trade unions, peasants' unions and women's and youth organisations claimed at least 10 million members. If the PKI had fought for the emancipation of workers instead of snuggling up to nationalists and capitalists, it could have led its mass following to challenge for power. Instead it left itself vulnerable to attack. The crunch came with a small failed coup on 1 October 1965, which the military falsely blamed on the PKI. The army, led by a little known Sukarno-appointee, General Suharto, then organised a counter-coup with the backing of the US, Britain's Labour government and Australia, and unleashed one of the worst massacres the world has ever seen. The PKI was unprepared and remained to the end unwilling to break with Sukarno and what it believed were 'pro-people' elements in the army. On 10 October, while its supporters were being rounded up and executed, the PKI's Central Committee instructed all members to 'fully support the directives of President Sukarno and pledge themselves to implement these without reserve'. In the face of such submission, the organisation was destroyed in the violence that followed. Every single one of its leaders was executed. Hundreds of thousands of members were slaughtered, the names of many supplied by the CIA. Virtually every radical element in the country was eliminated, either by death or imprisonment.

For the West, the new Indonesian president Suharto was a hero who had smashed Communism and would slavishly serve imperialism. The importance of Suharto's victory to the imperialist powers was summed up by Richard Nixon in 1967, a year before he became US president: 'With its 100 million people and its 300 mile arc of islands containing the region's richest hoard of natural resources, Indonesia is the greatest prize in South East Asia.'

The US and Britain ensured that for the next three decades their man in Jakarta was never short of the weapons of repression. US companies supplied 90 percent of the arms used by the Indonesian army when it invaded East Timor. The following year the US doubled military aid to the country whose invasion of a neighbouring state had been condemned as illegal by the United Nations. Between 1982 and 1984 it supplied the dictator with $1 billion worth of weapons. Even when Congress restricted military training and arms sales to Indonesia in 1992, the Clinton administration found ways of circumventing the restrictions. Meanwhile, both Labour and Tory governments in Britain ensured that Hawk aircraft, Scorpion tanks, water cannon, and a huge range of guns and other weapons were supplied, with payment guaranteed by the British taxpayer. New Labour's 'ethical' foreign policy made no dent in the sales: even as the Suharto regime lashed out with British weapons against Indonesians protesting against growing poverty in early 1998, sales of British weapons, including Hawks, continued unabated.

From the moment of Suharto's victory, Western multinationals also feasted on the profits to be made in Indonesia, particularly after their man opened up oil, gold, tin, copper and rubber for joint profit making ventures. As the country industrialised, the multinationals brokered deal after deal, always through Suharto's family and his cronies, to make money out of sweatshop labour and the financial system. Factories sprang up everywhere producing goods for export, goods such as trainers that sold for the equivalent of three or four months pay of the workers who made them. In the boardrooms of Indonesia's conglomerates men and women were feted by Western businessmen who now condemn them as Suharto's cronies.

For more than 30 years Suharto was hailed by the West as a genius who had painlessly modernised his country and brought wealth to his people. It was true that Indonesia had experienced strong economic growth (average annual growth of GDP was over 6 percent throughout the 1980s and 7.6 percent between 1990-95). Annual growth in income per head did average 4.6 percent from 1965 to 1996, increasing per capita income from $270 to $1,080, and there was a general fall in absolute poverty and an expansion of the middle classes.[2] But none of Suharto's Western admirers would admit that most of the wealth went into the pockets of Suharto's friends and the multinationals, and that the economy was already beginning to show signs of weakness because of cronyism and intensifying competition from other exporters in the region. They certainly didn't advertise the awkward findings of the UN Development Programme, which showed that in 1990 nearly 15 percent of the population would not reach their 41st birthday, that 38 percent of the population lacked access to safe water, that 15 percent of people lived on less than a dollar a day, and that in 1995 half a million children died before their first birthday.

The 'miracle' of Indonesia's economy was not as it appeared on the surface: economic slump was just around the corner. And the people who had suffered so much repression and exploitation on the promise of endlessly expanding national prosperity were about to explode in anger.

Economic crisis

By 1997 Indonesia's economy had grown to become the twenty-third largest in the world. But its long boom was beginning to falter. The reasons for the decline were similar to those affecting all the Tiger economies in South East Asia—rapid growth based on low wages and excessive borrowing, followed by overproduction, falling profits and debt crises. Indonesia's problems were particularly bad because its exports were being squeezed by Japanese competition in the more sophisticated goods and Chinese competition in the less sophisticated goods. Even its low labour costs were suffering from competition: companies such as Levi Strauss and Nike were finding even cheaper labour elsewhere. The particular problems faced by Indonesia were also partly caused and certainly exacerbated by Suharto's intransigence, greed, corruption and control of much of the economy.

Forbes, the US magazine, put Suharto third in its 'king or tyrant' category in 1997, estimating him to be worth $16 billion and his whole family $46 billion.[3] The family controlled most of the main conglomerates in the country, including Citra Lamtoro Gung Group, Bimantara Group and Humpuss Group, ran around 100 'charitable' foundations, and had shares in more than 1,200 companies. Among the industries they dominated were car manufacture, chemicals, media, telecommunications, hotels, shipping, gasoline, airlines, retailing, construction, toll roads, power plants, real estate and water.

Alarm about the Indonesian economy became public in August 1997, when the rupiah was allowed to float and Bank Indonesia introduced high interest rates. The following month the rupiah began to freefall, as did the stock exchange. The government froze infrastructure projects, but couldn't stop the rot. In October the World Bank, IMF and Asian Development Bank offered Indonesia a $37 billion rescue package, the second largest deal in history. Still the problems mounted. In November 16 banks closed and thousands of people's savings were frozen. Suddenly everyone began to notice that all was not well with the recently praised Indonesian economy. In late 1997 Western investors started complaining that the cost of paying off Suharto's family and cronies was adding up to 30 percent to some deals. A diplomat said at the time, 'They have started the feeding frenzy before the downfall.'

The international ruling class began to turn against Suharto. It was becoming increasingly impatient with the corruption of Suharto's ruling elite, which had become an intolerable barrier to the free exploitation of the Indonesian economy by multinationals and was provoking a potentially infectious uprising in the region. Their frustration was summed up in the IMF package, which insisted on the dismantling of all state sanctioned monopolies and restrictive trade practices.

By the beginning of 1998, the rupiah had collapsed to 10,000 to the dollar (from 2,400 in August 1997) after the budget breached IMF terms. Almost overnight the true extent of the crisis became apparent. Foreign debt stood at $200 billion, rather than the official $117 billion. Private sector debt was around $65 billion. Up to 80 percent of corporate Indonesia was technically bankrupt. Now Suharto had no choice but to turn to the IMF, which offered a $43 billion recovery package, attached to an 'austerity programme' and the scrapping of 12 major infrastructure projects. Suharto was not used to such treatment from his Western patrons, who were in effect asking him to dismantle his family's economic empire. He did everything he could to avoid implementing the IMF's demands, believing he would get the money in the end.

By May 1998 the rupiah had lost 80 percent of its value in a year. Imports, including rice and other key produce that Indonesians depend on for survival, became ruinously expensive. One industry association estimated that imports dropped from a pre-crisis level of $2.5 billion per month to around $100 million by early 1998. Foreign exchange reserves almost disappeared and the central bank began to print money recklessly, threatening hyperinflation. Most of the country's 200 commercial banks were exposed as illiquid, and some could not cash cheques. The huge foreign debt could no longer be serviced without rescheduling. The level of domestic debt was bringing production to a standstill. Even the massive state owned Pertamina, the oil and gas monopoly, defaulted both domestically and abroad, and was forced to halt production.

Ordinary Indonesians were being made to pay for the $43 billion IMF bail out, but the Suharto family (which was worth almost the same amount as the bail out) was being let off the hook. When the government announced in early May 1998 that electricity and petrol subsidies would have to be removed to save 27 billion rupiah, some Indonesian newspapers asked why the government had been able to find 103 billion rupiah to rescue the banks owned by its cronies so easily. The rupiah's exchange rate crash meant the oil industry was making superprofits overnight, yet none of the benefit was being passed on to consumers. Such disparities fuelled unhappiness about the glaringly obvious inequalities between classes and regions. The ratio between the highest and lowest income groups rose from 3.8 in 1985 to 6.2 in 1993,[4] and rose even more sharply in the following years. The eastern part of Indonesia, accounting for 40 percent of the land area, was receiving only 7 percent of private investment. The new office blocks, luxury department stores and other signs of wealth in Jakarta were standing side by side with slums: nearly half the population in the capital had no drinkable water or primary health services. A few miles from the modern cities were peasant communities hardly touched by the 20th century—a classic example of what Trotsky described as combined and uneven development.

As the crisis deepened, survival for the masses became increasingly hard. Food prices were soaring while wages were frozen. In less than a year the price of rice had risen by 38 percent, cooking oil by 110 percent, chicken by 86 percent and milk by 60 percent. Subsidies that are the difference between life and death for millions of Indonesians were being cut or threatened. Basic goods and medicines were in short supply. And every day people were being laid off as companies crashed. From January 1998 onwards, an average of more than 2 million workers lost their jobs each month. On top of all this, there was a crippling drought related famine in vast areas of the country, and an additional million children faced being withdrawn from school because their parents could no longer afford the fees.

In early May the situation deteriorated further as the IMF 'reforms' began to bite. Train fares were doubled and it was announced that electricity prices would go up by 60 percent and water rates by 65 percent. The price of fertilizer, crucial for millions of people in the countryside, had risen by 12 percent in a month. Everywhere people were getting hungrier and poorer by the day.

Political crisis

The deepening economic crisis was being matched by a growing political crisis. Suharto was facing a people who had slowly and painfully begun to recover from the terrible defeat of 1965. The first major sign of the revival of resistance came in 1974 when a million people spilled onto the streets during widespread student protests. The most significant development, however, was the emergence of a huge working class. Tens of millions of people had been drawn into manufacturing and other industries, where they were exploited at incredible levels. Yet they were also brought together as workers, and as the 1980s progressed they began to use their collective strength to strike for better wages and working conditions with some success.

In 1973 trade unions had been forced to merge into a federation whose president was a former military intelligence officer. Despite this, some sections of the federation still tried to represent workers' interests, so the government replaced it in 1985 with the All-Indonesian Workers' Union (SPSI), which was dominated by business people and Golkar representatives. Faced by mounting illegal trade union activity, the government was forced to end the ban on strikes in 1990, after which the number of strikes rose steadily. In 1995, 365 strikes were registered. In 1996 the number rose to 901, nearly three a day, involving around half a million workers.

By 1997 there were 20 million workers in the major urban centres, with a further 66 million workers elsewhere. Around 30 million were working in the service and minerals sector.[5] According to Suharto's government, 74 percent of foreign exchange earnings were derived from the non oil and gas sectors: of this, manufacturing contributed more than 63 percent. Women were particularly affected by the migration to the towns. By 1997 they made up around 40 percent of workers, compared with 33 percent in 1980. Most worked in the worst factory jobs, often in special export zones, where they made up nearly 90 percent of the workforce.

Women became increasingly prominent in strikes and as union leaders.

Despite the very real economic gains made by workers (manufacturing wages rose by an average of 5.5 percent a year between 1970 and 1991), their wages were still pitiful, even compared to other developing Asian countries. The average wage was 20 US cents an hour in 1994 compared to 54 US cents in China.

Although the level of strikes rose, the political consciousness of workers remained low. Most strikes were confined to immediate economic demands, such as wage increases to the legal minimum level, or transport allowances. In 1993, after Marsinah, a young woman active in an industrial dispute, was brutally murdered and mutilated a wave of strikes spread, building support for the new independent trade union SBSI (the Indonesian Prosperous Trade Union) which had been formed in 1992. In February 1994 Muchtar Pakphahan, the SBSI's leader, called a nationwide one hour strike and thousands of workers took part. A month later there was an explosion of strikes in Medan, the country's third largest city, which led to still more daring demands. The SBSI organised a virtual shutdown in the city involving tens of thousands of workers walking out of 70 factories. The demands included big wage increases, the right to organise and operate through the SBSI, an investigation into the death of Marsinah, and government intervention to reinstate 380 workers sacked at a match factory. As a result of the action, Muchtar Pakphahan and many other SBSI activists were thrown into jail. In 1995 another independent trade union, the PPBI, was formed, led by a 23 year old woman, Dita Sari.[6] It organised many strikes in textile and other factories. Its leaders were jailed too, including Dita Sari for six years.

By 1996 dissatisfaction with the Suharto regime was spreading to sections of the ruling and middle classes, who were being excluded from the profit and corruption bonanza by Suharto's cronies. Even Megawati Sukarnoputri, the timid daughter of Sukarno and leader of the Indonesian Democratic Party (PDI), one of the two parties 'authorised' by Suharto, began to speak out. Her mild criticism won immediate and enthusiastic mass support. So Suharto fostered a rival PDI faction led by Suryadi, who was then 'elected' PDI leader in June 1996. When the new leader tried to take control of the party headquarters in July 1996, Megawati's supporters barricaded themselves inside the building, while mass rallies were held outside, bringing together a wide range of opposition forces. On 27 July the military attacked the headquarters, sparking off widespread riots in Jakarta. The crowds burned down 22 buildings, including police and army offices, banks and luxury car showrooms.

In the following eight months hundreds of political activists were imprisoned and popular discontent increasingly disintegrated into attacks on ethnic minorities. The gloom was shattered by a new surge of activity before and during the rigged parliamentary elections of May 1997. Mass demonstrations involved hundreds of thousands of people. Protesters broke through army barricades. There was widespread rioting, particularly by the urban poor and the youth. Up to a million people occupied the streets in parts of greater Jakarta on at least two occasions. Radical anti-Suharto slogans emerged and towards the end of the campaign open street fighting broke out.

Protests at varying levels were mounting throughout the country. They included strikes, large demonstrations, and attacks on police stations and government offices. In April 1997 a wave of strikes erupted across the industrial belts of Jakarta and Surabaya in protest at the minimum wage level. Then Nike workers went on strike for four days, beginning with a 10 kilometre march by 13,000 workers. After management reneged on an agreement which had brought the Nike workers back in, a second, more violent strike began. Workers smashed all the windows of the company and destroyed cars. The demands, albeit minimal ones, were suddenly met. In June bus drivers struck for two weeks in Jakarta and Bogor, causing widespread chaos. The strike quickly spread to cities across West Java and elsewhere. The same month the Barbie doll factory was shut down by strike action until workers' demands were met.

The authorities responded with increased repression, particularly of trade unionists. In September 1997, for example, security forces raided the SBSI's Congress, arresting 13 people, including foreign delegates. But they could no longer stifle union activity. In October workers at two major companies, IPTN (aerospace) and PT PAL (shipbuilding), staged huge strikes. The 16,000 workers at IPTN won a major victory over wages and other demands after a showdown with the boss, one B J Habibie who we shall meet again soon. Banners strung on the walls during mass meetings read: 'Sack the corrupters and increase wages by 200 percent' and 'Bosses enjoy the good life, workers live in misery.' In November 40,000 workers at the prestigious Gudang Garam clove cigarette factory went on strike for four days and won almost all their demands, including a 50 percent pay rise.

1998: countdown to victory

From the beginning of 1998, rioting and demonstrations spread across the 13,000 island archipelago. In January, the main form of protest was strikes. In February riots dominated, particularly in Java. From March, student protests took the lead, culminating in mass demonstrations and devastating riots in May. But throughout this period, all the forms of protest were happening at once. In fact, a classic revolutionary situation arose: the ruling class was no longer able to rule in the old way, and the ruled were no longer prepared to tolerate their rulers.

The rioting, fuelled by hunger, rising prices and unemployment, was spontaneous[6], disorganised and violent. Because the people involved lacked any collective base or political leadership, much of the anger was initially directed at Indonesia's ethnic Chinese community. This racist response to the economic crisis was stoked up by the government and by the main Muslim groups. On 9 February, for example, Suharto told a well-publicised meeting of Muslim leaders that 'outsiders' (Chinese) were responsible for the economic crisis. The same month Amien Rais, chairman of the 25 million strong Muslim movement Muhammadiyah, publicly blamed rich Chinese 'parasites' close to Suharto for the crisis. This followed the exposure of a document written by Special Forces Commander Prabowo Subianto, Suharto's son-in-law, which called for a campaign to blame Chinese businessmen for the financial mess.

In this climate, ethnic Chinese traders in the villages dealing in staple goods became easy targets for hungry people. In the towns large supermarkets and luxury goods shops owned by ethnic Chinese were blamed for high prices. On 9 February, for example, ethnic Chinese shops and businesses on the eastern island of Flores were burned down and looted. In Pamanukan, a large town just 95 kilometres from Jakarta, days of rioting beginning on 13 February destroyed shops, restaurants, churches and schools associated with ethnic Chinese. There were also horrific mass gang rapes of Chinese girls and women, and many attacks on poor Chinese residential areas.

However, much evidence has come to light since early 1998 that such attacks were orchestrated and carried out directly by the military. Small groups of men, either having the appearance of soldiers in civilian dress or accompanied by people in military uniform, arrived out of the blue in Chinese areas. They daubed houses with anti-Chinese slogans, encouraged people to join assualts they had started on terrified Chinese people, and invited men to participate in gang rapes. They also went through the streets shouting out anti-Chinese slogans, using language that exactly replicated anti-Chinese government propaganda.

Ethnic Chinese make up less than 4 percent of the population but control around 70 percent of the wealth. Twelve of the 15 wealthiest families are Chinese.[8] The vast majority of ethnic Chinese, however, do not belong to the billionaires' club and struggle even harder than most Indonesians to make ends meet because of state sanctioned discrimination. As early as 1967 Suharto's government set out its 'Basic Policy for the Solution of the Chinese Problem'. Chinese newspapers were closed down. The use of Chinese characters in public places was banned.

Chinese language schools were shut. Ethnic Chinese were banned from joining the military or government, and excluded from many state universities. They even had to carry special identity cards.

This 'solution' reflected the fact that ethnic Chinese have had a similar role in Indonesia to Jews in Europe in the past. Under the Dutch colonialists the ethnic Chinese were traders while the indigenous population was forced to work as slaves on large plantations. As the country industrialised, richer ethnic Chinese largely took over banking. They also bought hotels, department stores, factories, restaurants and many other businesses. At times of economic or political crisis, they have persistently been scapegoated by the authorities, as were Jews in Europe. During the mass killings that followed the military coup in 1965, ethnic Chinese suffered terribly, and Suharto and his friends regularly stirred up racist hatred in the following decades. The Muslim organisations also tried to gain support by vilifying 'Christians' (many ethnic Chinese Indonesians are Christian), or by stigmatising the Chinese explicitly. The main victims have been the poor ethnic Chinese: the rich learned from 1965 and most moved their main residences and much of their money abroad.

The rioting in early 1998, however, was not directed solely at ethnic Chinese particularly in areas where the working class was strong. In fact, as the crisis deepened, the focus of protests shifted towards the government and symbols of the ruling class (which did sometimes include Chinese businesses), especially when the protests had an organisational base such as student campuses or workplaces. In the industrial heartland of Surabaya in East Java, for example, violence spread through the city after riot police attacked student demonstrators in early January. Here banners were held aloft, saying 'Reduce prices, smash the seat of power'. There was little sign of racism. In the following days, nearby cities were engulfed by riots, starting in Banyuwangi on 12 January and then moving on to Jember and Pasuruan. Shops were looted indiscriminately and security forces drafted in stood by unable to stop the waves of destruction.

Despite a total ban on all meetings and protests, and mass deployments of troops in the major cities, rioting and pro-democracy demonstrations spread like wildfire across the archipelago, and some strikes were held. In January, for example, workers in many factories went on strike when bosses refused to pay traditional holiday bonuses. Every day another group of protesters arrived outside parliament to air their grievances.

In February rioting broke out in at least 25 towns in east and central Java, Sumatra, Sulawesi and Flores, provoked by rising prices. According to Amnesty International, security forces responded in some areas with live bullets. Two people were shot dead in Brebes, Central

Java, and two on the island of Lombok. Hundreds of protesters demanding political reform were arrested around the country as Suharto called on the military to take 'stern action' against demonstrators. On 12 February he said, 'We cannot let them [demonstrators] hide behind the veil of democracy and freedom to express their opinions and then make good on their destructive and law violating ways'.[7] Students responded by pouring out of Jakarta's University of Indonesia and Yogyakarta's Gadjah Mada University to demand more political freedoms and human rights. Some students held hunger strikes.

On 11 March Suharto was 'elected' to his seventh consecutive presidential term, with B J Habibie as his vice-president. The 1,000 member People's Consultative Assembly—500 appointed by Suharto, 500 vetted by him—did not even hold a vote. There wasn't much point as Suharto had not allowed anyone else to stand. Opposition leaders Megawati and Amien Rais decided to do nothing to upset the election ceremony, apparently willing to go along with Suharto's month-long ban on all public meetings and demonstrations. Students reacted differently. The main campuses throughout Java erupted and student protests spread across the country. Lectures were cancelled and campus life across the archipelago became one long political meeting punctuated by angry demonstrations.

The activity was reflected in a proliferation of student newsletters across the country. The first and most prominent one, *Bergerak!*, was launched on 10 March at the University of Indonesia after a 1,500 strong rally. The four page daily was crammed full of news of student rallies, legal advice on the rights of demonstrators, interviews with activists, and satire directed against the authorities. Each issue sold out instantly.

As the student protests grew, army chief General Wiranto and education minister Wiranto Arismunandar warned students not to take the protests off campus. They were ignored: days later students took over the streets in Solo (Surakasta), central Java, and in two Sumatran cities. General Wiranto offered to talk to the students, but they refused, demanding to see Suharto instead. Many student activists were arrested and some disappeared, presumed dead. By April the clashes between students and police were growing steadily more violent. Students began throwing molotov cocktails and rocks at security forces, and set vehicles alight. In Yogyakarta police were injured and their cars smashed. Campuses became battlefields, surrounded by water cannons and bombarded with teargas.

On 11 April General Wiranto again warned students to stay off the streets, threatening more violence. A week later student leaders met cabinet ministers, following which Suharto ordered the army to be ruthless. Immediately riot police began firing rubber bullets. Every day more activists disappeared with a few reappearing telling stories of torture at the hands of the military. But each round of violence garnered support for the students. 'Workers, professionals, housewives, even nuns began joining the students,' reported *Asiaweek*.[10]

At the start of May Suharto announced that democratic reform would not be introduced until 2003, when his term was due to end. Students reacted immediately and organised increasingly large demonstrations. After some rallies on campuses students tried to take to the streets. Sometimes they managed to break through security force lines, and thus won much support from workers and the city poor. When security forces blocked students on campus, they provoked violent clashes, sometimes sparking off riots in nearby areas.

The temperature was raised further in early May when the government announced it would implement the IMF's requirement to stop subsidising fuel and electricity prices. Immediately the cars of the rich and their chauffeurs began queueing for petrol, gridlocking the streets in some cities and forcing the poor to walk home—another sign of the rich being untouched by the 'reforms' while the poor suffered. On the morning of 4 May a huge student demonstration filled the streets of Medan. As soon as that was over, the city exploded into rioting, which lasted for three days. 'Crowds formed, then rampaged. If troops or plain-clothes police appeared, there would be a clash, or the crowd would dissolve down Medan's streets and alleys followed by teargas and bullets. What they did not take, they torched'.[11] Troops closed the toll road. No ships left nearby Belawan harbour. Hundreds of shops were ransacked and similar numbers of cars left smouldering. Chinese shops and homes suffered worst. The bewilderment felt by the poorer ethnic Chinese was expressed by a 48 year old salesman: 'We eat here, we sleep here, we even shit here—why can't we be accepted?' By the end of the three days, at least six people had been shot dead by troops and several had died in blazing stores. Hundreds of people were arrested, but most were released soon after. Riots breaking out elsewhere were also being met by security force violence. In Yogyakarta, for example, a young unemployed engineer who was simply watching rioters was beaten to death by soldiers.

Then workers began to stir. In the first week of May a wave of strikes broke out in the industrial estates to the west of Jakarta. Around 2,000 workers in ceramic and chemical plants in Tangerang and Serang struck, demanding wage increases to keep up with inflation. Some 1,200 workers at Surabaya's P T Famous plant walked off the job.[12] Around 2,000 medical staff from Surabaya General Hospital demonstrated, demanding democratic reform. Mass demonstrations and riots were now breaking out across the archipelago, including in all the major towns and provincial cities. It was the beginning of the end of Suharto.

Ten days that shook Indonesia

On 12 May the spark was lit that ignited the capital, Jakarta. Six students demonstrating outside the University of Trisakti were shot dead. Dozens were injured. The attack by the security forces was sudden and unprovoked, and no doubt ordered by the hardline element in the army under Suharto's son-in-law Prabowo in a last ditch attempt to frighten people back to their homes. Around 5,000 students from Trisakti, one of the country's most prestigious private universities, had been demonstrating against Suharto. They were blocking traffic as soldiers stopped them marching to parliament. For hours there was a stand off. At 5pm the students negotiated a solution: one row of students would back off for every row of police that did the same. But then suddenly the security forces charged, shooting into the ranks of the students with plastic and live bullets. From daybreak the following morning, thousands of students began arriving in delegations at the college, as did leaders of the democracy movement. Megawati spoke for the first time since the protests began. Amien Rais spoke too. Both called for non-violence, but it was too late.

An Australian socialist was there: 'Students began to drift into the streets. Here they were joined by workers, the unemployed, the poor. Around Atmajaya University, in the heart of the city, office workers left their desks and came into the streets to express their support for the students. By nightfall, riots were spreading and the following day saw Jakarta in flames. Few corners of greater Jakarta were untouched. It was impossible to get to the airport, difficult to go anywhere. Some neighbourhoods looked like war zones'.[13]

For three days Jakarta was overwhelmed by protests, riots, looting and attacks on buildings. Vast numbers of the capital's poor rioted, stealing what they could carry, burning and destroying anything that smacked of authority. Most stole food and clothing, which had become unaffordable in recent weeks, or 'luxury' goods such as televisions and refrigerators that had always been beyond their means. The violence was both random and directed. People tore down traffic lights and also smashed banks and cash machines belonging to the Suharto family. They threw stones at any window that was unbroken, yet concentrated on symbols of wealth. They set fire to buildings but worst hit were those associated with Suharto's family. Vast crowds demolished car showrooms owned by Suharto's son Tommy. They burned down the social affairs ministry, run by Suharto's daughter Tutut, and torched the toll booths her company had built. They ransacked a house owned by Liem Sioe Liong, one of Suharto's closest friends and Indonesia's richest man. They burned his fleet of flash cars and slashed his portrait. The chant of 'Down with the King of Thieves' rang out.

Alongside the riots, demonstrations of students and workers were continuing. Although virtually unreported, they were large and met with gunfire by the security forces. One victim was 21 year old Teddy Kennedy, the son of a parking attendant, Roy Effendi, who had chosen his boy's second name in honour of the US president. Teddy had joined one of the demonstrations and was killed by a bullet in the back of his head fired by the security forces.[14]

For the urban poor who made up the majority of the rioters, there were few other ways of expressing their anger. They had no college campus to occupy or student delegation to join, no factory to occupy or strike to organise. They were unemployed or eking out a living in small unorganised sweatshops. Many were provincial migrants, recently uprooted from their villages with no links in the city. Every day they faced harassment and abuse by police and officials. Arifin Hanif, one of the newly unemployed, had been held for two weeks in 1996 and tortured by soldiers. When the riots came, he saw his chance: 'This is the sort of situation I have been waiting for'.[15]

On their own the riots would have led nowhere. But because they had been sparked by the wider discontent, they quickly stoked up the political crisis facing the ruling elite.

As Jakarta burned, claiming hundreds of lives,[16] the military stood by. Many soldiers sympathised with the protests. Troops who were called to secure Indofood's Jakarta distribution centre, for example, helped the looters. The company's marketing manager watched the soldiers ask rioters to line up for merchandise and heard them saying, 'Once you've got enough, please go outside and give other people their chance'.[17] Security forces who arrived after people set fire to a branch of Liem's Bank Central Asia simply warned the rioters not to stand too close to the flames. In many places demonstrators chatted with soldiers, putting flowers in their guns and pleading with them to side with the people.

People who were rioting also began to play an explicitly political role. Outside the National University they urged students occupying the campus to take to the street and actively join the uprising. The students refused, saying they were against violence! On the streets photocopied lists of Suharto's family's assets were being sold for the equivalent of 10 US cents. One crowd of rioters rained missiles on a police station and then set fire to it. 'Police, come out and face us', they shouted.[18] The *Jakarta Post* reported someone who was supposed to be part of a 'mindless mob' screaming out, 'The government should realise that the price of fuel must be reduced'.[19]

As the rioting spread across Jakarta, schools and businesses closed. Buses and taxis stopped running, particularly the previously ever present dark blue Citra cabs owned by Suharto's daughter Tutut. 'They knew that if they went on the streets they would have been torched,' said a cab driver. Middle class families put signs outside their houses hailing the martyrs of Trisakti University. Rich Chinese families as well as employees of foreign companies and international organisations fled to the airport. Military trucks began picking up people stranded by the riots and taking them home.

By 15 May, Jakarta was like a deserted battlefield. Few people ventured out. Most businesses were shut and currency trading was halted. Vast areas had been reduced to rubble—in all, the destruction was worth about a billion dollars. More than 5,000 buildings had been destroyed or damaged. At least 500 bank branches and 200 cash points had been trashed. Hero supermarket, the largest chain in Indonesia, lost 25 of its 40 outlets in the capital. Whole factories, including the Unilever factory in the eastern suburbs, were burned down. Meanwhile, protests were intensifying in other parts of the country. In Yogyakarta, students clashed with security forces, threw molotov cocktails and stones at police lines, and burned photographs and effigies of Suharto. Students also took a member of the local parliament hostage. In this city police responded with teargas, rubber bullets and water cannon.

Significantly, in the major industrial centre of Surabaya, where students and workers joined forces, the security forces were passive. Students stormed the radio station RRI and forced their demands to be broadcast while thousands of people kept guard outside. Elsewhere in the city rioters attacked the provincial legislative office. Security forces closed off streets but not a single shot was fired.[20] As a result, yet more activities were organised. The *Jakarta Post* reported, 'About 4,000 housewives, female students, factory workers, activists, nuns and prostitutes gathered at the Airlangga University and held a free speech forum where they voiced support for the student movement for reform'.[21] Rioting and student protests erupted in practically every major city across the country.

The reverberations of the protests reached Cairo, where Suharto was meeting other rulers during the G15 Summit of developing nations. He flew back to Indonesia on 15 May, apparently thinking that if he asked a few unpopular cabinet ministers to resign, especially his daughter Tutut and his close friend Mohamad 'Bob' Hasan, the protests would end. His parliament seemed loyal enough. A few hours later he had lost much of its support. The House Speaker, Harmoko, one of Suharto's most trusted allies, turned on him, calling on him to resign 'for the sake of national unity'. Harmoko's words were too late to save his house, which was being burned to the ground as he spoke.

Meanwhile, the protests intensified. Thousands of student protesters in the Central Java capital of Semarang, joined by hundreds of workers, took over the state owned radio and forced the station to air their demands for reform. Violent clashes between students and police broke out in Surakarta, Central Java, Bogor, West Java and in Medan, where the students sat down and held a free speech forum as they blocked the traffic. They also sang anti-government songs and posed for photographs with soldiers.[22] In Purwokerto, Central Java, over 3,000 students tried to break through a police barricade and were only driven back by teargas. In Bandung, West Java, nearly 100,000 students from colleges all over the province occupied Gedung Sate, the centre of the provincial administration and the provincial council.

The authorities then seemed to realise that Surabaya was a key battleground. A special reserve force headed by Suharto's son-in-law Prabowo was deployed to confront the might of the city's huge workforce and student population. It roared through the city firing on demonstrators, lashing out with rattan canes and wooden clubs. A *Guardian* journalist described one of many incidents: 'This time the shooting was in response to angry onlookers throwing stones at a lorry-load of the hated strategic reserve troops over the road. The military driver stopped, turned his vehicle and drove straight across the central reservation and headed straight for the stone throwers'.[23] Later, just after the military had agreed to negotiate with student protesters, the military suddenly opened fire: 'There had been no provocation. But the green bereted strategic reserve seemed to have no compunction about turning its guns on those protesting against Indonesia's aging autocrats.' As a result of the military's violence, rioting and looting spread, and 2,000 students marched to the provincial council building.[24]

The country was now visibly at war with itself, with cities encircled by military armoured cars and soldiers guarding government buildings. By 18 May it was clear in the capital that something mighty was happening. Students marched into the main parliamentary building, where members were still sitting, and handed out pro-democracy bandannas to the men and women placed there by Suharto. Many of those who for years had done everything in their power to suppress democracy then donned the symbol of democracy. Outside, students were fraternising with soldiers, encouraging them to support the ordinary people. For 32 years parliament had simply been a temple to Suharto: no debates were ever heard. With the students in occupation it was suddenly at the heart of political change.

By 19 May up to 30,000 students were occupying parliament and the security forces were doing nothing. Buses kept arriving, bringing delegations of students clothed in their college colours. Students climbed onto the roof to unfurl banners. A huge cheer went up when a thousand labour activists arrived to add their voice to the call for change. 'We want Suharto and Habibie to stand down,' said Datuk Bagindo, chairman of the official trade union federation, SPSI. 'Because of the economic crisis caused by Suharto's administration, workers are facing mass dismissals, lay offs and the worst hardship'.[25]

The students inside parliament were typical of student occupiers the world over. They were at once exhilarated and politicised by their daring and terrified of what might happen to them. A 40 metre long banner hung from the roof read: 'Return sovereignty to the people. Thirty two years is enough.' Inside the building the air was heavy with the smell of clove cigarettes. 'In the library, students shredded and burned documents. Someone smashed the glass door to the presidential washroom. Students made out on the lawn'.[26] There was also the consuming fear of another Tiananmen. 'They lived from hour one with the paranoia of a crackdown, rumours lumbered through the humid air, and, more than once, word came that soldiers were poised to burst in, wielding death,' reported *Asiaweek*.[27] The protest was infecting everyone in the city, even stockbrokers. Around 300 stopped work for 20 minutes at the Jakarta Stock Exchange and chanted, 'Step down Suharto'.

Still Suharto tried to play for time. He announced a cabinet reshuffle and suggested new elections 'sometime soon'. Then he said he would not stand in them. But even that was not enough. Harmoko's call for him to quit was supported by three other former vice-presidents. Then 13 ministers resigned.

For several weeks all the opposition had been preparing for mass demonstrations on 20 May, the 19th anniversary of National Awakening Day which commemorates the birth of Indonesia's nationalist movement. In town after town, village after village, buses and coaches had been booked to take people to marches. A million people were expected to gather at the national monument square in central Jakarta, not far from where Suharto was hiding.

As the momentous day approached, General Wiranto ordered thousands of troops and tanks into and around the capital. Then, on the eve of the protest, he warned that the military would tolerate no further disturbances and would shoot 'looters' (demonstrators) on sight. He had a quiet word with Amien Rais, reminding him of the Tiananmen Square massacre in China on 4 June 1989. As the evening of 19 May began, soldiers cordoned off the square with barbed wire and declared it a forbidden zone. By daylight thousands of troops had sealed off the city with light tanks and armoured personnel carriers. As the sun rose further in the sky on National Awakening Day, busloads of students began arriving at parliament to join other students who had spent the night there. People lined the street to welcome them, chanting, 'Suharto must go.' Middle class people turned up with food, cigarettes and water for the students. Expectations were high. Everyone was nervous. Today was showdown time.

But then Amien Rais stepped in. He went on national radio and television to urge the people not to march. He said he was afraid of massacres by the army. This was a reasonable fear, given the military's track record, and was shared by many. But the truth was that Rais was more afraid of the prospect of a million fired-up people gathering in the city and getting out of control. Unfortunately, most people in Jakarta listened to him as there was no other organisation that could give the lead and mobilise people who had shown they were prepared to risk violence in order to win reforms. And so the momentum was lost and the chance of immediately pushing the revolution to greater heights evaporated. In the capital National Awakening Day turned into a day of respectable people gathering at parliament, including Rais, business people and many professionals, to make one demand only: Suharto must go.

In some places outside Jakarta, Rais's call for people to stay at home was ignored. In Suharto's home town of Yogyakarta, for example, up to a quarter of a million people took control of the streets. In Surabaya huge demonstrations by workers and students were violently broken up by troops. By the evening it was clear that Suharto was on his way out. The head of his own ruling party gave him a blunt ultimatum: resign or face impeachment. Even General Wiranto was demanding that he go so that he could be replaced in a 'constitutional' and orderly fashion. Any further delays might threaten that possibility. The army chiefs pleaded and begged, promising him that they would defend his life and property to the death. Finally Suharto conceded.

At 9am the next morning, on 21 May, Suharto resigned in a televised broadcast: 'I am of the view that it is very difficult for me to carry out my governmental duties. I have decided to cease to be President of the Republic of Indonesia effective immediately.'

The dictator had gone! A mass movement had ousted him. Everywhere the people cheered and celebrated their victory. Unfortunately, all power did not go to the people cheering, but to Suharto's best mate and former vice-president, B J Habibie—the man who called his erstwhile mentor SGS (Super Genius Suharto).

After the uprising

One of Habibie's first acts as president was to order security forces to clear parliament of the remaining student protesters. On 22 May they stormed the building armed with teargas, clubs and machine guns. There was no resistance. It appeared that the 'moderates' had won and now people would settle down to see what Habibie could deliver. Pretty soon, however, it became clear that Habibie was incapable of dealing with the many crises he faced. The economy was still in freefall and he was trapped by his unwillingness to attack the Suharto family's business empire and his fear of the far from pacified populace.

In the weeks after Habibie took office, the rupiah kept falling: by 12 June it had crashed to 14,850 to the dollar, a 20 percent fall in a week. There was also a massive run on the Bank Central Asia and the government was running out of money: the central bank's reserves were down to around $7 billion. The much needed next tranche of the IMF's $43 billion bail out due to arrive in July would be a drop in the ocean given the scale of debt and the collapse of industries. Unemployment kept rising and was forecast to reach 15.5 million by the end of the year, about 17 percent of the workforce. Inflation, which had already reached 52 percent by June, was predicted to rise to 80 percent by December.

The enormity of the economic problems was undeniable. Almost everyone agreed that the economy would contract by around 20 percent during this year. In the towns and villages, food supplies were running out and anyway were becoming unaffordable. Even if enough could be imported at the higher costs, disrupted distribution systems once run by ethnic Chinese firms were raising prices further. In addition, economics minister Ginandjar Kartasasmita said in June that government subsidies of basic food goods (including flour, sugar, corn, soya beans and fishmeal) would be completely lifted in October, as required by Indonesia's agreement with the IMF.

In an attempt to distance himself from the regime that spawned him, Habibie raised the possibility of seizing some of the Suharto family profits and investigating corporate corruption. Not surprisingly, he has so far done little to follow this up. Any investigation would quickly lead back to Habibie himself and many of his ministers—all major stakeholders in companies connected with Suharto. Foreign companies are also reluctant to dig up the dirt, as they are almost exclusively established in Indonesia because of sordid deals with Suharto and his cronies.

The close connection between the state, banks and industry in

Indonesia, which had been one reason for the economy's rapid expansion, was now part of the problem. The state's control of banking and industry had allowed firms to enter international markets from which they would otherwise have been excluded by international competition, defend themselves against technically more advanced rivals, and survive periods of low profits while entering established markets. The state's involvement also protected imports through tariffs, provided incentives to exporters, and developed the infrastructure and education needed for the development of a modern economy.[28] In addition, the repression combined with a total absence of welfare provision forced workers to save, aiding high levels of investment.

The financial crisis was caused by the age old capitalist problem of too many goods being produced for demand, increased competition, and falling rates of profit. Left to its own devices, capitalism would allow the weaker capitalists to go under—firms would close, banks would collapse and savings would be wiped out—until the system was ready for another round of expansion. This process began happening so dramatically in Indonesia because for years Suharto's corrupt state had propped up banks and bailed out companies that would otherwise have collapsed. So Habibie faced a harsh choice: further economic decline or the conditions laid out by the IMF. But these conditions mean restructuring banking and industry, ending tariffs, opening up the economy to Indonesia's competitors, and stopping subsidies (risking further revolts), none of which appeal to the Indonesian ruling class.

Pressure from the IMF as well as continuing protests at home soon began to force the issue. In June relatives of Habibie, Suharto and General Wiranto were resigning almost daily from positions they had achieved by nepotism. Huge contracts with foreign companies, including Thames Water, were being cancelled or reviewed to stem the accusations of corruption. On 4 June the *Jakarta Post* editorial read: 'The fury directed against Suharto, stoked by the almost daily reports uncovering his huge business empire, may run out of control to the degree that people may look to take the law into their own hands.' It continued: 'We cannot afford this kind of frenzy because it would literally affect just about every sector in the economy, since it is being discovered that Suharto's family and cronies are engaged in businesses ranging from satellite communications, power, toll roads and printing to oil and gas, transportation, food, pharmaceuticals, petrochemicals and plantations, to name just a few.' It might have added that Habibie has his claws in around 80 major companies and corporations.

The resignations did not even begin to touch the economic problems that were increasingly affecting millions of Indonesians through job cuts, falls in real wages, rising prices and food shortages. Industrial workers were living off the equivalent of less than 50 US cents a day, and the average per capita income had fallen in a year from $1,200 to $300. Hunger and homelessness faced millions of people in both the cities and the countryside. According to Rekson Silaban of the SBSI union, there were about 150 million people living below the official poverty line.

Such conditions were fuelling the other major problem facing Habibie—continuing social unrest. It quickly became clear that students and workers, bolstered by their recent success and newly won freedoms, would not suffer in silence to allow Suharto's best mate to protect the interests of the rich while doing nothing for the poor. Each 'concession' granted by Habibie to appease popular anger, such as the release of political prisoners, appeared to generate more activity, not less. After he lifted the ban on opposition parties (excluding socialist or communist organisations), political parties began springing up daily. Crucially, workers were being drawn into struggle as they were forced to defend their livelihoods in the face of closures and cuts, and each time they took action they were still facing the might of the military—a strong reminder that even basic democratic reforms had still not been achieved.

One of the first new parties to be formed, the Indonesian Workers Party (PBI), was organised by labour activists in order to challenge for power in any forthcoming parliamentary elections. Sri Bintang Pamungkas, the day after his early release from prison, announced that he would register his long outlawed organisation, the Indonesian Democratic Union Party (PUDI). Feminists got together to found the Indonesian Women's Party, declaring their aim was 'to empower women in the political field'. Even the ruling Golkar split, with new parties peeling off.

In early June thousands of workers demonstrated outside the manpower ministry demanding the legalisation of independent trade unions. Habibie obliged by lifting the ban on such unions. The employer who had made so much from suppressing trade unionism promised that his government would never again use military interference in labour disputes and would respect workers' rights to strike when fighting for their interests.[29] His words had an immediate effect, even though his promise about the military's role was quickly broken. Muchtar Pakphahan, who had just been released from prison, registered the SBSI and announced that the union would continue its fight to strengthen workers' bargaining power. Thousands of workers went on strike in many factories across Surabaya and staged huge and violent protests in the streets. They were demanding up to 50 percent wage increases to keep up with spiralling inflation. Thousands more workers from electronic and machinery factories near Jakarta demonstrated to stop job losses. A demonstration of staff at the national airline, Garuda, demanded cancellation of contracts linked to the Suharto family. And the parliament in Jakarta once again became the focus of student protests, with around 5,000 rallying outside to call for more reforms.

Around the country, people emboldened by the May events organised to express long felt grievances. In Purwokerto in Central Java, for instance, 200 farmers rallied to demand the resignation of the village chief who had embezzled their money, while on a vast area of land owned by Tutut which had been cleared for development in north Jakarta, hundreds of slum dwellers staked their claims, driving signs with their names into plots they believed they were reclaiming for Indonesia's *orang kecil* (small people).

By the end of June more workers had mobilised. Thousands from three factories demonstrated outside Surabaya's local parliament. Around 3,000 workers from the Victory Long Age shoe factory demanded pay rises, menstruation leave and tax relief. Some 1,500 workers from two timber factories demanded the sacking of two bosses and pay supplements. On 25 June 1,000 members of the SBSI union rallied in Jakarta calling on Habibie to resign. Some 7,000 workers at the Tryfountex Indonesia factory in Solo went on strike between 30 June and 4 July to demand higher wages and other fringe benefits. After management threatened mass sackings, workers set up an independent Workers' Committee for Reform (Komite reformasi Kaum Buruh), which among other things called for their factory to be nationalised. The committee also declared that workers should not confine themselves to immediate economic demands, and invited student leaders to address the workforce.

Another political minefield also confronted Habibie. In occupied East Timor tens of thousands of people attended meetings to demand independence. In Jakarta a large demonstration on 12 June calling for East Timorese independence was broken up by police. This was the first use of violence by the security forces since the May uprising and showed that the state was still the same beast that had terrorised the nation for 32 years, albeit with a new face as its president.

Habibie tried to soften the government's stance on East Timor, offering a limited degree of autonomy some time in the future. But this just fuelled anger. No doubt the issue of East Timor will cause further violence: the government knows that success for the East Timorese independence forces would encourage secessionist movements elsewhere, including Irian Jaya, Aceh and oil rich East Kalimantan.

All over the country, there were increasing signs of class polarisation, as there had been in the days leading up to 21 May. Banners raised at various protests called for Habibie to go, complained at the lack of reforms, and demanded property to be seized from the rich and returned to the people. Tensions were apparent within the student movement between those who believed the overthrow of Suharto was enough, and those who wanted democracy and major economic reforms introduced immediately. Some students wanted solidarity with workers; others rejected such solidarity. Workers were striking for wage increases and to build their own unions, and were being politicised by their constant confrontations with the military. Sections of the middle and ruling classes were meanwhile mobilising to show their support of Habibie and to call for calm. The country was in revolutionary turmoil, but there was no revolutionary leadership.

The forces challenging for power

The appointment of B J Habibie in place of Suharto seemed to be the perfect interim solution for the sections of the ruling class that had wanted the least change possible to diffuse the protests. He was a creature of Suharto—a senior government minister since 1978 and intimately linked with Suharto and his cronies of old, including timber king 'Bob' Hasan, and Suharto's son-in-law Prabowo, leader of the most ruthless element in the army. Habibie was best known for the ludicrous money guzzling aircraft industry he established to produce Indonesia's own aeroplane, the useless N-250. Money was diverted from the government's reafforestation fund to bail out the company, and Merpati Airlines and the military were forced to buy Habibie's substandard products. He also has extensive interests in 80 companies linked to government projects, state owned and military run enterprises, and affiliated banks. This is spearheaded by the $60 million Timsco Group, run by his youngest brother, which has its hand in chemicals, construction, real estate, transport, communication and joint ventures with the US telecommunications giant AT&T. Military leaders backed Habibie's appointment as they felt he offered the best hope of restoring order and protecting the military's economic interests. On top of the enterprises it seized after independence, the military has established companies and extended its control over state owned corporations such as Pertamina, the oil giant; Bulog, the state food distribution network; and Berdikari, the official trading group.

The temporary installation of Habibie also suited liberal opposition leaders such as Megawati and Amien Rais, who did not want the uprising to get out of control and needed time to prepare for what they hope will be peaceful elections. Megawati, once the great hope of liberal democrats, has proved cowardly and ineffectual. Until the killings at Trisakti, she said nothing. Then she appealed for calm. Soon after Suharto was toppled, she made only her second high profile speech to urge the nation to 'show compassion and stop battering fallen president

Suharto'. A member of the Indonesian elite, she has been paralysed by her terror of the masses. She has repeatedly declared her support for the existing constitution which, among other things, entrenches the army as the dominant political force. She is a fan of Western capitalism and has long been closely associated with those demanding a rapid transition to a free market policy based on private capital and competition.

The main beneficiary of the May uprising was Amien Rais, chairman of the vast Muslim movement Muhammadiyah. A US-trained academic, he won considerable support among students during the protests and came across as a decent liberal. The truth about him is less pleasant. In 1988, for example, the military encouraged him to condemn ethnic Chinese as traitors who were to blame for unrest, thus allowing pro-government Islamic leaders to cheer him on and call for all good Muslims to support Suharto. He was also a leading figure in the powerful Muslim Intellectual Association (ICMI), established in 1990 by Habibie with the backing of Suharto. ICMI is a focus for non-Chinese or *pribumi* businessmen who resent the influence of wealthy ethnic Chinese families.

Rais's class allegiance was fully exposed on 19 May when he called off the mass rallies scheduled for National Awakening Day. Like Megawati, he represents sections of the ruling class who missed out on the gravy train, as well as intellectuals and members of the middle classes who want liberal democracy but are nervous of mass struggles. Both he and Megawati were among the first to support the IMF's intervention and conditions, and both have the support of the international ruling classes, who fear further damage to some of the biggest companies in the world—BP, Shell, Rio Tinto, General Electric, Siemens, NEC, Hyundia and BHP—which have joint ventures with members of the Suharto elite. Since 21 May, Rais has bent over backwards to prove his credentials to his Western admirers. He backed Habibie's appointment, stressing their personal friendship. He said he did not think the new president would be Suharto's puppet. 'If somebody is intelligent enough to make an aircraft, I hope he is intelligent enough not to be a puppet leader,' he told journalists.[30] Soon after, in early June, he told a mass student rally that debates on the legitimacy of Habibie's appointment 'should stop'. Everyone should calm down and wait for elections, whatever the delays.

Megawati and Rais are a barrier to further reforms that are so deperately needed to ease the suffering of the masses. Not only have they failed to mobilise people who were only too ready to fight, but they have also poured cold water on those who had joined the struggle. Rais was honest about his fears as far back as February 1998, when he told an ABC interviewer, 'Mobilising people is easy, but controlling them is difficult.'

The perceived wisdom expounded by Megawati and Rais, and

accepted by many in the reform movement, is that all Indonesia's problems are due to 'crony capitalism'. Once the cronies are removed, so the argument goes, then capitalism in Indonesia will once again flourish. The truth is that no section of the Indonesian bourgeoisie, however liberal sounding, will be able to carry out the measures required to even begin to tackle the inequalities, poverty and economic crisis in Indonesia. For that to happen, some of the enormous material resources would have to be taken from the elite and the multinationals and given back to the people, and major political and social reforms would need to be introduced. Those leading the opposition have no desire to do this, and even if they did, the full might of the army would be mobilised to protect not only their political role in the country, but also their material wealth.

As has been demonstrated above, the key political force for change in the run up to May was the students. Half the Indonesian population, around 100 million people, are aged under 20. They do not remember 1965, have been angered by the lack of free speech and repression, and are fearful of the lack of opportunities they face as the economy crumbles. Although they were crucial to the events leading up to Suharto's overthrow as they sparked much wider protests, students alone cannot and will not change Indonesian society more radically. Most come from relatively privileged backgrounds and their demands are limited. More importantly, students alone, however radical, do not have the power to overthrow the ruling class.

However, students have shown Indonesians that mass action can win, and have raised expectations about justice and democracy in the country. To make even more progress, especially on the economic front, organised labour needs to be mobilised and politicised. If they use mass strikes and factory occupations to voice political as well as economic demands, then the ruling class would come under intense pressure. In the process of such collective action, a political movement independent of liberals such as Megawati and Amien Rais could be developed. Key to that process is the working class and the left.

During the protests that led up to 21 May, the workers were relatively passive. The main reason was the shadow of unemployment which hung over every factory. As the economy disintegrated, millions of workers were laid off—thrown into instant poverty in sprawling slums where they had few, if any, family ties. According to the Indonesian Writers' Syndicate, more than 16 million industrial workers were laid off in the six months up to May. Those still in work were desperate for the wage packet that would stave off hunger.

The other reason was the absence or weakness of trade union and political leadership. Independent trade unionism had only begun to grow in the past few years so its roots were weak and its presence uneven across the country. Moreover, its leaders and activists still faced the most brutal repression right up to the May uprising. When Suharto fell, most of the leaders of independent trade unions and hundreds of union activists were in prison or had been killed.

The weakness of the left was again a legacy of the years of repression, but also of the disastrous experience of the PKI in the 1960s. No independent revolutionary socialist organisation exists, even in embryo form. The most radical organisation is the People's Democratic Party (PRD). Despite being condemned by the government as 'Communist', it is in fact a radical reformist organisation. Its main demand has been for a 'people's coalition government' rather than a socialist revolution, although some of its members are socialists. It was formed in April 1996 and almost immediately the PRD and its affiliated organisations were banned by Suharto after the protest outside the PDI office.[30] Most of the leaders were arrested, including PRD chairman Budiman Sujatmiko and Dita Sari, head of its affiliated independent trade union PPBI.

The PRD worked in alliance with Megawati's Indonesian Democratic Party (PDI) and recently focused its efforts on the urban poor rather than organised workers in an effort to promote 'popular radicalism'. Nevertheless, the PRD demands self determination for East Timor and is undoubtedly militant—one of its slogans is 'Look for the fire, fan the fire'—and has organised workers to take industrial action. In early 1998 the PRD was extremely small given the scale of events, having only a few hundred members and a few thousand supporters. Most of its core activists are students and former students. But its calls for the overthrow of Suharto and its pro-democracy slogans appear to have gained it much support.

In the current climate there are huge opportunities for the left to prosper. One reason is that the situation remains incredibly volatile. Firstly, the effects of globalisation mean that countries such as Indonesia are vulnerable to currency speculation, the flight of capital and intense competition from neighbouring countries. Combine this with the organic crisis of Indonesian capitalism and the deepening regional and world economic crisis and it is clear that there is every chance that Indonesia will continue to slide deeper and deeper into recession, with devastating effects for the mass of Indonesians. On the political front, the lack of effective democratic and legal institutions means that the authorities have few tools to channel the spirit of reform. Similarly, the absence of established social democratic or Stalinist parties and the weakness of the trade union bureaucracy to moderate and mediate struggle also makes the situation potentially explosive. In such a climate, the current leaders of the reform movement may be quickly exposed.

On 1 June, for example, dozens of red and white banners appeared on the capital's main streets with the names of the best known opposition leaders. But there were also slogans that would terrify those same leaders: 'People are starving! Take back people's money.' If the economic situation continues to worsen, the contradiction between the aims of the liberal leadership and the needs of the people will become ever clearer. If a socialist voice could be organised and heard, it would quickly gain support.

During the May 1998 events the whole country apart from Suharto's clique was united around the call for greater democracy. But the 'democracy' was ill defined and meant different things to different classes. For Megawati and Rais, democracy means a greater ability for the ruling class to benefit from a free market. They are much like the leaders of 'People's Power' in the Philippines, who in the end brought little but further economic suffering for the masses. If people such as Rais are put in power, the story will be much the same. They will be compelled by the IMF and others to use methods every bit as ruthless as Suharto to implement 'reforms' whose main consequence will be worsening living conditions for millions of Indonesians.

For workers, democracy only means anything if it brings better living standards and health care, an end to ethnic and racial discrimination, and freedom to organise and agitate for socialist demands. Habibie certainly won't deliver such reforms. But neither will Amien Rais or Megawati. Real changes that would genuinely improve the lives of the masses will only be won if they are fought for by workers, students and the poor. Their success will depend on whether they organise independently and adopt a socialist strategy.

Notes

1. Golkar stands for Golongan Karya (functional groups) and incorporates the bureaucracy, the education system, local neighbourhood administration, and a set of parallel organisations. Along with the military, it is in effect the state.
2. Figures in 1996 dollars.
3. Figures for 1997 as reported in the *Financial Times*, 19 May 1998.
4. Indonesian government figures.
5. M Mlah, 'Repression and Revival', *Against the Current*, January-February 1998.
6. Since May the Indonesian and international press has been claiming that the riots were instigated and orchestrated by sections of the military as part of an internal battle for power. Although there is evidence that some units did stir up violence against ethnic Chinese and carried out rapes of Chinese women and girls in May, such incidents do not explain the widespread and mass rioting, which in most cases was spontaneous and an expression of popular anger against the regime.
7. The PPBI is affiliated to the People's Democratic Party (see page 27).
8. *Asia's Wealth Club: Who's Really Who in Business—the Top 100 Billionaires in Asia* (Nicholas Brealy Publishing Ltd).
9. AFP, 12 February 1998.

10 *Asiaweek*, 22 May 1998.
11 Ibid.
12 *Kompas*, 7 May 1998; *Suara Merdeka*, 6 May 1998.
13 Australian *Socialist Worker*.
14 *The Guardian*, 16 May 1998.
15 *Asiaweek*, 29 May 1998.
16 Indonesia's National Commission on Human Rights estimated that 1,188 died. The military claimed 500 lives had been lost.
17 *Asiaweek*, 29 May 1998.
18 *Jakarta Post*, 14 May 1998.
19 Ibid.
20 *Jakarta Post*, 16-17 May 1998.
21 Ibid.
22 Ibid.
23 *The Guardian*, 21 May 1998.
24 *Jakarta Post*, 14 May 1998.
25 *Jakarta Post*, 21 May 1998.
26 *Asiaweek*, 5 June 1998.
27 Ibid.
28 C Sparks, 'The Eye of the Storm', *International Socialism* 78 (London, 1998).
29 *Jakarta Post*, 5 June 1998.
30 Among the groups affiliated to the PRD are: the Indonesian Centre for Labour Struggles (PPBI); Students in Solidarity with Democracy in Indonesia (SMID); the National Peasants Union (STN); the Surakarta Peoples Union (SRS); and the Jakarta Peoples Union (SJ).

Sex, class and socialism

Lindsey German

Daily we are bombarded with images of women as sex objects, housewives and mothers. As we approach the 21st century women face a backlash against the gains they have made. The political right, backed by a new generation of post-feminists, stress women's role in the home. Lindsey German explains the most recent developments and examines the various theories which try to explain women's lives, including the theory of patriarchy, which has shaped much feminist thinking. She looks at the patterns of women at work, how the family affects women's lives and how women have organised to fight for their liberation.

With women under attack and the women's movement in disarray, *Sex, Class and Socialism* is a crucial contribution to this fight.

£7.95, available from Bookmarks, the socialist bookshop
1 Bloomsbury Street, London WC1B 3QE
Phone 0171 637 1848, fax 0171 637 3616
email bookmarks_bookshop@compuserve.com

BOOKMARKS PUBLICATIONS

Three interviews with workers' representatives and socialists in Indonesia

Interview with factory representatives of the Workers' Committee for Total Reformasi (COBAR)

International Socialism: **What impact did the May events have in your workplace?**

Male stationery factory worker, Kapuk (Jakarta region): After things happened in May the military came to the factory to try and prevent the workers joining the political activity. After the riots and demonstrations the employers shut down the factory and asked the workers to guard the factory. So they were not doing their real work but just guarding the factory.

Woman clothing factory worker, Kapuk: After the riots my factory was being guarded by the military. Even the security guards were not allowed to continue their jobs.

IS: **What were your workmates saying about the demonstrations and riots?**

Woman kitchen goods factory worker, Kapuk: The workers kept hearing the news on TV and they supported the students because they also wanted a new leader. And after Suharto stepped down, they were hoping for a better government.

Male timber plant worker, Lam Pung (Sumatra): After Suharto stepped down, the minister of manpower said there is freedom to join workers' federations. But in a concrete way, when workers in the factory try to build such a federation, then the military try to stop them. So it is still difficult to build in the factories because the military try to scare workers, even though the minister of manpower said that we have the freedom to build such federations.

Woman clothing worker, Kapuk: The workers in Kapuk supported the demonstrations because they wanted a new government and because it seemed that they had a freedom of speech which they did not have before. But during the riots the employers told the male workers to guard the factory. After two weeks they even offered to let people go on the pilgrimage to Mecca. The direct effect of the riots is that basic necessities become very expensive and scarce.

***IS:* Did people in the factories support the riots of the urban poor against the state?**

Woman clothing worker, Kapuk: Sometimes, they didn't always support the looting of the stores because it's a lottery and they live on very low wages. They didn't necessarily support the attacks on the big stores.

***IS:* What was the attitude to attacks on the Chinese? Were there arguments against attacking the poor Chinese?**

Male stationery worker, Kapuk: Workers supported the transformation process, but not in the sense of stealing from the Chinese. They don't support the anti-Chinese movement. A lot of Chinese do have economic power, but there are also Chinese people who have become integrated with Indonesian people. So it would be wrong to have an anti-Chinese attitude.

***IS:* Was there contact between students and workers?**

Male stationery worker, Kapuk: Not yet.

***IS:* Have strikes increased since the overthrow of Suharto?**

Male timber plant worker, Lam Pung (Sumatra): Yes, obviously. In my workplace there have been a lot of workers' struggles against the employer. In June there were about 20 factories in struggle in my town. These were all strikes. In Sumatra the economic crisis has become deeper and the workers' response has been to strike. This week there have been seven strikes and there will be more next week.

Male stationery worker, Kapuk: In Suharto's time there was a lot of military intervention. People didn't get their holidays and wages. So people are demanding their wages, their rights, and an end to military intervention. The demands are political as well as economic.

Male pharmaceutical plant worker, Lam Pung (Sumatra): In Sumatra the demands are to raise wages and to stop unemployment and to stop military intervention. They also want an end to Law 25, so allowing freedom of trade union organisation.

IS: **Many of the trade union representatives here are women. Are women's issues and issues of equal pay being raised?**

Woman clothing worker, Kapuk: There has been discrimination for years. One of our demands is to stop the pay discrimination between men and women. At my factory we produce bras for companies like Triumph. There is an issue of sexual harassment. The company insists that we wear transparent uniforms on the factory floor so that they can see we are not stealing bras. At the end of each shift we are searched. Many of the women are Muslim and the security guards and management are male.

IS: **What would the representatives here regard as real democratic change? What would have to happen for such change to be a reality for them?**

Woman kitchen goods factory worker, Kapuk: Real democracy must come from the people. Workers should have their representatives in parliament. Workers should have a national organisation. There should be representation from many different sectors in the new regime.

Male timber plant worker, Lam Pung (Sumatra): The leaders should come from the people, not from the elite.

IS: **People seem very dissatisfied with Habibie. Will people accept the present situation? Can Habibie survive?**

Male pharmaceutical factory worker, Lam Pung (Sumatra): Habibie is bad because he likes to spend a lot of money. Habibie is part of the cadre of the old regime. If we want democracy we must overthrow this regime and replace it with a new leadership drawn from all sectors.

Male shoe factory worker, Kapuk: Habibie is a technocrat. He doesn't really know about people's economic problems so he can't lead the people in this economic crisis.

IS: **How does COBAR organise?**

COBAR organiser: The COBAR organiser in Kapuk was a worker at first, then he became a full time organiser because his factory was burnt down in the riots. The way we organise is by building the confidence of our friends to fight the employers, by pamphlets and newsletters. COBAR has already built contacts in a factory and has a co-ordinator in each factory, so when COBAR wants a strike we call the co-ordinator and discuss what they want to do, and the co-ordinator asks the workers to take action.

IS: **What are the demands of the strikers?**

COBAR organiser: During the last strike wave the demands raised depended on the individual factory's policies. But although different factories have different specific demands, they all strike at the same time.

IS: **Is there 100 percent support for the strikes?**

COBAR organiser: Recently nine factories were on strike at the same time and five had total support with all the workers out on strike. They were fighting for specific concessions from their own employers, but all fighting at the same time. For example, in one photo album factory the workers struck for money for meals and transport. In another factory they had already won these so they were striking for other things.

IS: **Do the women union representatives organise male workers too, or do they just represent women-only factories?**

COBAR organiser: Some women representatives are in factories where the majority of workers are women. But it is not a problem if women are the representatives in factories where both men and women work.

IS: **Would people here consider themselves to be socialists?**

Male timber plant worker, Lam Pung (Sumatra): Yes, you could say that. I want our country to become a socialist country.

Interview with POSKO (student based organisation) member at the University of Indonesia, Jakarta

IS: **How did your organisation relate to the first wave of demonstrations on the campuses?**

The demonstrations began before the presidential elections. They started in March and February because people were so angry with Suharto. The crisis in Indonesia meant that the movement increased in size. Two weeks before the presidential election most of the movement said 'No to Suharto' and general strikes broke out in all cities and especially in the University of Indonesia. There was a general strike of students, but not only among students. The students said 'No to Suharto' and the movement spread because the bigger universities in every city in Indonesia, in Jakarta and elsewhere, organised strikes and smaller campuses followed their example. Then in every city we built coalition organisations, but it never became a national alliance of students. When we realised that Suharto would be given power again by Congress the movement did not stop. On the contrary, it became bigger. It reached its peak when our friends in the university in west Jakarta were shot. Six students were shot dead and others are still missing. After that there was an explosion of anger amongst the people and riots broke out in every city in Indonesia, especially in Jakarta. On 13 and 14 May Jakarta was reduced almost to anarchy, with people burning buildings and looting shops. In addition, anti-Chinese feeling grew up everywhere.

IS: **Did your group organise in one particular campus?**

Yes, in the University of Indonesia.

IS: **How did you begin to organise there?**

We have a tradition of organisation in the university, so we have established an atmosphere where social and political problems are always being discussed. Almost every year we organised little strikes, which is why when the crisis really began to bite the strikes erupted more regularly. We organised when the new students came to the campuses every new term, by showing them the oppression which exists in Indonesia. We organised big discussions and after about a month of education we broke up into small discussion groups. The raw materials of the movement came from these groups.

IS: **What do you discuss?**

Everything—we discuss national issues and conditions and we have ideological discussions to educate students in Marxist ideas on politics and economics. We stood for the student council and used those positions to organise. In May we argued that students had to build links with the urban poor and with workers. We won that argument on our campus. People came to address our mass meetings. But when it came to the student occupation of the parliament building the leadership of the central co-ordinating committee were carried away with the image built up of the students, in the press and by sections of the military and government, that somehow student protests were legitimate. They not only argued to keep the urban poor and the workers out of the occupation but they organised a cordon to enforce that decision.

From our campus we organised to smuggle the urban poor into the occupation on board our buses. But when we handed out a leaflet arguing for unity the leadership of the occupation called on people to tear it up. I addressed the occupation about this but they shouted me down. But it was clear that there was a polarisation. When it was announced that Suharto had stepped down there was immediate jubilation. But then those students who supported Amien Rais argued that Habibie's appointment should be welcomed because he was a good Muslim. Others were not happy that Habibie had been made president. When the universities go back in August we expect this process of polarisation to grow. It is important that we continue to build on the campuses.

Interview with full time COBAR organiser

IS: **What is the relationship between students' and workers' struggles?**

The Department of Manpower had a strike. Over 1,000 workers went on strike for a whole year, but the non-government organisations kept on hoping that the workers by themselves would organise spontaneously. In response to the worsening conditions of the 1990s, students organised demonstrations to government buildings and even to parliament, then workers copied these demonstrations and copied the tactics the students used, such as producing posters showing the demands they were fighting for and organising big rallies. Before, workers only knew how to strike, but they tried to learn from the students.

IS: **Is the strike movement continuing and are some of the strikes political?**

Almost every day there are strikes, and some of them are political strikes. The political demonstrations are the organised demonstrations; the spontaneous demonstrations are rarely the political ones. Until 1990 the working class increased in size until there were about 10.5 million workers in manufacturing alone. Also there is a situation where a lot of workers come from the country and villages and there is a threat of mass deportations back to the country which is used to prevent people from getting involved in politics.

IS: **Is the historical comparison more like the 1905 revolution in Russia than February 1917, so this is more like the beginning of revolutionary organisation in Indonesia?**

We have established discussion groups, which talk about the capitalist system, but at first the students just wanted to discuss politics, not to organise the workers. A minority of the workers have become political, but they are separated from the other workers. But also in the 1990s most of the organisations in the big factories organised big demonstrations, and they encouraged other smaller factories to do the same. So the situation in the industrial areas becomes explosive: workers are not afraid to have demonstrations and other groups of workers get involved.

IS: **So the movement spread along the lines Rosa Luxemburg described in *The Mass Strike*?**

The problem is that the workers have not made really good progress; it is the student groups who attempt to bring politics to the workplaces. They make a little progress and then they move to other workers to set up a discussion group, so there is no real leadership over economic problems and no real consistency.

IS: **So they remain as discussion groups?**

So when the demonstrations spread in the industrial areas, the students still limit their activity to organising discussion groups. Also the student groups have not progressed much either, so the students just jump from one issue to another and it becomes hard for them. They use lots of energy but don't build anything. Meanwhile there has also been an increasing political crisis in the government so other sections of society are beginning to address wider issues, but the majority of workers still see their own boss as the main problem.

IS: **Is this changing now with the depth of the economic crisis?**

Yes, workers are beginning to look increasingly to political issues beyond their own workplaces.

IS: **Are the urban poor still attacking buildings?**

No, that only happened on one occasion, in May. Now they are waiting for another chance.

IS: **How do you see the future of Habibie? Do you think it is a stable regime?**

His party has elections in November. We think Habibie will not be the leader after November because he is not accepted by the people or the military.

IS: **So you think it will be a long term crisis, an organic crisis?**

It is a global crisis, as well as a deep crisis in Indonesia.

IS: **How do you see the democratic revolution in relation to the socialist revolution? Do you think there is a separation?**

The socialist revolution and the democratic revolution are not separate. The process of insurrection can lead to rapid change, or to slow gradual change.

IS: **If the regime falls through mass action, could that open the door to rapid transformation?**

Yes, that is why we are trying to build a democratic coalition in Indonesia, involving groups that do not have the same ideological positions as us.

IS: **With what sort of groups are you working?**

For example, if people from Amien Rais's organisation wanted to work with us, we would not refuse them. We want to build the biggest possible coalition for democratic reform.

IS: **Do you think Rais would support that?**

No. Megawati may, but not Rais.

IS: **Why do you think Megawati has been so quiet and careful?**

Megawati is an ambiguous figure. She never makes a catagorical statement. But she is supported by the people because of her father. Megawati stays a long way behind the masses. They are running ahead calling her on.

IS: **Is she still the most popular opposition leader?**

Yes, she has the support of most of the people. That is the stupidity of Megawati, because if she dared to take the leadership, she could do it. And because of her lack of a political background, she is just a spoilt child, and some in the movement call her a housewife.

IS: **In the Philippines Cory Aquino moved quickly to stop the revolutionary process but here, because Megawati has been so slow, it means that the process can become more protracted and much deeper.**

Yes, we agree.

IS: **How do you see your organisation developing from here? What is your immediate perspective?**

From the past of our movement, we have learnt to concentrate on other sectors of the country. In Jakarta we put out a political leaflet arguing 'Down with Suharto. Take his wealth. Lower the prices'. Now we are concentrating our efforts on the workers, because the workers move slower than students but they are better organised. Also we have programme for students to go and organise the workers, put out leaflets and so on.

IS: **The demand to take Suharto's wealth is a good demand—after all, it is all still there. Is it a popular demand with the masses?**

Yes, the masses would say it is a good idea.

IS: **Have you organised among women workers?**

Yes, about 60 to 70 percent of workers are women.

IS: **Are they well organised?**

Not in separate women's organisations, but in factory organisations, yes they are. They are the leaders of some of the unions, representing men as well as women.

IS: **Are the women more militant than the men?**

Yes, because the history of our movement shows that the factories with most women workers tend to be the most militant. The most active workers are the women workers. They regularly attend meetings and the representatives of each workforce are usually the most active workers in the factory, often women. The representatives always give speeches—it doesn't matter whether it is a man or a women. Also we try to build around issues important to women workers because the discrimination against women still happens. There is not equal pay and social conditions, so sometimes men get money for meals and women don't. There is also sexual harassment. Women often get body searched at work and they don't get menstruation holidays. In the middle class the issue of women is also being raised, because of the rape of Chinese women. Middle class feminism is also growing but because of exploitation most working class women look to workplace organisation, not middle class feminism.

IS: **Would you like to say anything to people in Britain?**

Yes, keep fighting. Let's fight for a classless society.

Report from Indonesia

CHRIS BAMBERY

The scale of the crisis which has overwhelmed Indonesia is enormous. The Indonesian government's statistics bureau predicts that almost half of the nation's more than 200 million people will be below the official poverty line by the end of 1998. The World Bank estimates it will be at least 2005 before per capita income recovers to its pre-crisis level.[1] Redundancies are mounting. The PT Toyota Astra Motor company has cut its workforce from 7,000 workers to just 2,500. Before the financial collapse Toyota Astra produced about 7,000 Kijang cars, Indonesia's most popular and least expensive cars. Car sales fell by 95 percent in June, from 38,733 cars sold in the previous June to just 1,833 this year.[2] Inflation in July 1998 was running at 56.7 percent according to government figures. It was forecast to reach 80 percent before the end of the year. On 1 August this year the Ministry of Manpower announced it would increase the minimum wage by an average of 15 percent. This was the first such increase since April 1997—before the collapse of the economy, before the rupiah collapsed and the soaring inflation that followed.

This is the background to the student protests which began in March when Suharto was re-elected president by 1,000 hand picked delegates at the People's Consultative Assembly and Golkar, Suharto's personal political machine, ensured B J Habibie's appointment as vice-president. It is also the background against which we must judge the stability of Habibie's government.

The May 1998 uprising of the urban poor remains as a reminder of the discontent which lies beneath the surface. On the road into Jakarta from the airport, two months after the riots, banks and car dealers remain boarded up. In the far south of the city the skeleton of a burnt out department store looms up into the night sky while further on stand the ruins of a bank. The governor of Jakarta reported that 4,940 buildings were damaged, burned down or looted. These included 4,204 shops, shopping malls, restaurants, car workshops and more than 500 bank offices. The Indonesian Retail Merchants Association estimated retail stores would lose 600 billion rupiah (US$60 million).

The Indonesian government estimated losses from damaged property in Jakarta alone at 2.5 trillion rupiah (US$350 million). The Pertamina oil company suffered damages of 1.5 billion rupiah, including damage to 12 petrol stations. The National Logistics Agency claimed that 1,800 tons of sugar and 500 tons of rice owned by the agency had been looted. Fourteen police posts were badly damaged in the riots. Three days of rioting left around 1,200 people dead.[3]

The rebellion of the urban poor was the decisive turning point. Panic swept the ruling class. A dozen US companies, including American Express, Boeing, Citicorp, Nike, Mobil, Mattel and McDonald's, shut down their offices in the capital. Mattel closed down two plants making Barbie dolls employing 7,000 and evacuated 100 staff from the country. On the Wednesday night after the riots the minister of security and armed forces commander, General Wiranto, visited Suharto's mansion to deliver a message from the Indonesian armed forces (ABRI) asking him to resign. The generals had reached their decision that afternoon.

Habibie's authority always depended on Suharto. He does not have a significant, independent political base. Prior to being appointed vice-president by the ousted dictator, he was president of the state owned aircraft manufacturer, PT IPTN, and the state owned shipyard, PT PAL. The industries under his control were targeted as among the most wasteful by the IMF. After being appointed vice-president, Habibie had his son replace him as president of PT IPTN. An opinion poll quoted in the *Jakarta Post* found that 46.42 percent of those asked found Habibie was acceptable but just 1.1 percent found him very acceptable. This poll gave a snapshot of middle class opinion. It means there is no large popular base for Habibie.

More importantly, it is common for people to describe Habibie as being Suharto's puppet. They think that the former dictator still pulls the strings. The ABRI operates as both the military and the civilian authority in the country. But in addition it controls key sectors of the economy. For instance, it has a major interest in plantations producing sugar, rice, palm oil and other crucial commodities, and each of its component parts—the army, navy, air force and police—have co-operatives operating in various business sectors. The Indonesian Co-operatives Council is actually dominated by representatives of ABRI owned co-ops. Beyond the military, the ruling Golkar apparatus continues to dominate the Habibie government.

But there are tensions apparent within the armed forces. At the beginning of August the commander of ABRI, General Wiranto, removed Lieutenant General Prabowo Subianto and Major General Muchdi Purwopranjoyo from their posts. These two commanders were suspended from their posts pending a probe into their role in the abduction and torture of democracy activists. Prabowo is Suharto's son-in-law and until March this year he headed the elite special force Kopassus, which was responsible for the kidnappings. His replacement was Muchdi. They and ten other officers of this elite unit will face a specially convened military tribunal which was set up a day after US defence secretary William Cohen visited Jakarta. Cohen and Bill Clinton's foreign secretary, Madeleine Albright, have all urged that ABRI should be reformed.

Suharto remains in Jakarta, living in his upmarket home in Menteng, central Jakarta. On 3 August the Austrian business daily *Wirtschaftsblatt* reported that Suharto had moved billions of US dollars to Austrian banks shortly before his resignation. This followed reports in the US business magazine *Barrons* quoting David Hale, the chief economist at Switzerland's Zürich Insurance, to the effect that Suharto had moved US$8 billion to Austria from Indonesia. According to *Forbes* magazine's rankings of the world's richest billionaires, Suharto amassed stakes in about 3,200 Indonesian companies during his 32 years in power and had a family fortune of US$4 billion. Other Indonesians included in the list were Eka Tjipta Widjaja of the Sinar Mas Group who was worth US$4 billion; the Wonodjojo family who own the Gudang Garam Group who were worth US$2.1 billion and Liem Sioe Liong of the Sudono Salim group who was worth US$1.7 billion.[4]

Meanwhile there is little sign that the economic crisis has bottomed out. The country's private sector foreign debt stands at US$84 billion. The public sector debt stood at US$54 billion in May. These figures rocketed following the 80 percent depreciation in the value of the rupiah. Following a deal brokered in Frankfurt in June the debt was rescheduled. But two months later no company had signed up with the new Indonesian Debt Restructuring Agency. The real issue will come when negotiations open between individual firms and their creditors. A senior analyst at a foreign investment bank in Jakarta explained:

> The debt deal struck in Frankfurt is largely meaningless. Companies simply cannot pay, even under the terms agreed in Frankfurt. Creditors must realise

they have no option but to write off a lot of their loans, try to come to an agreement with companies that can be salvaged, and get back what they can.

The World Bank in its latest report on Indonesia admits the bulk of Indonesian owned firms are being literally crushed under a massive burden of external and domestic debt.[5] Indonesia is among the world's leading exporters of tin, copper, nickel, gold, coffee, cocoa, tea, palm oil, coconut oil, rubber and plywood. But against that the country has to import rice, wheat and sugar to feed its 200 million population. This year Indonesia is set to import a record 5 million tons of rice.[6] In the wake of Suharto's fall, the head of Asia Pacific research at CIBC in Singapore said, 'Aside from political reforms the economy is going to be the one that is much harder to turn around and it's going to get a whole lot worse before it gets better.'[7] Economist Sri Mulyani from the University of Indonesia told the *Jakarta Post*, 'There is a feeling that political support for President B J Habibie and his government is so thin that he cannot launch an adequate agenda for political and economic reform.' Regarding the immediate economic outlook she warned:

Indicators like inflation and employment show that the economy has not reached the bottom of the crisis. It's now very difficult for us to stop the economy from deteriorating even further because of the government's negligence when the crisis first broke... Habibie has sent out conflicting signals. For example, he said he would eradicate corruption, collusion and nepotism but he has not yet introduced any legislation to achieve this end. Abolishing such practices is very important because they are merely the tip of an iceberg of structural problems that include a poor bureaucratic system, an excessively close relationship between the government and business, and the societal role played by the military. These structural problems drove Indonesia into the current crisis.[8]

A snapshot of the situation in Indonesia is provided by a glimpse at news reports on just two days in late July.

On 22 July the new government of Habibie announced it will give Suharto over US$2 million as a housing allowance. On the same day farmers seized the headlines worldwide by invading a golf course near Jakarta and planting seed before being evicted by riot police. On 23 July the *Jakarta Post* reported 12 democracy activists had been abducted and tortured by an elite military unit. In the same issue it reported that 800 pharmaceutical workers in Tangereang in Jakarta had struck for union recognition and reinstatement of their factory representative. Meanwhile the headline on the front page announced that 'Tycoons Support Habibie'.

During the May protests the leaders of the student movement used the term *reformasi*, reform, in an effort to find a term acceptable to the government and the ABRI. But what they were actually demanding was something stronger than mere reform. The slogan 'reformasi' was never defined and so it has taken on very different meanings for different sections of the population. The Habibie government seeks to cloak itself in the slogan. For instance, the government called on people to grow more vegetables. But that statement was cited not just by the farmers who ploughed up the golf course but by others of the rural and urban poor who grabbed vacant land earmarked for luxury housing developments. Every day there are official statements bemoaning the thefts taking place from shrimp farms near the capital. On 17 July President Habibie opened a market in central Jakarta selling cheap food and other goods to the poor. He bought a pair of shoes worth US$3.20 claiming that while he once bought expensive imported shoes he has now cut back because of the financial crisis. Within an hour of Habibie leaving, the poor simply walked off with all the cooking oil on offer. Two weeks later 100 people seized a 3,000 square metre site in east Jakarta earmarked for luxury housing in order to plant vegetables. The land was owned by the state. A spokesman for them said, 'Most of the people intending to grow vegetables work as *mikrolet* [minibus] drivers or have no job at all. It's better for us to be involved in such a project rather than killing our time by playing cards or stealing amidst the crisis.'[9]

A process of polarisation is now developing among those who seemed to stand together against Suharto in May. Mochtar Mas'oed, a lecturer in political science at Gadjah Mada University in Yogyakarta, explained:

> In rural areas reform is even misunderstood as disobedience toward the authorities. Thus the word reform has become meaningless in line with the changes in the political situation, while pro-reform activists who were united by the common issue of leadership succession, have disintegrated following the downfall of Suharto on 21 May. It is very difficult now to unite them because each of their factions has its own agenda and priorities.

At the time of the student occupation of the parliament buildings there was a sense of elitism among the student leaders that somehow their protest was dignified and peaceful, unlike that of the urban poor, and a sense too that the students were being feted by the media and by sections of the ABRI leadership. But a process of polarisation began as soon as the dictator was removed. When Suharto fell, student supporters of Rais welcomed Habibie's appointment on the grounds that he was a good Muslim. The chair of the Association of Muslim Students, Anas Urbaningrum, stated:

We should give Habibie a chance. Let him prove that he can solve the problems of the country. We should not judge him before giving him a chance.

This contrasted with the mood among other activists. A student at Bina Sarana Informatika told the *Jakarta Post,* 'We reject Habibie. We want Suharto's regime to be purged from this nation.' Another student at Jakarta Economics Academy said, 'He can't rule the country as Suharto is still behind him.'[10] As the universities return in August this debate will intensify.

The most popular figure in Indonesia is undoubtedly Megawati, the daughter of the former president, Sukarno. Yet she played a very cautious role during May and did not rush to place herself at the head of the protests. That allowed Suharto to hand over office to Habibie. But the fact that Megawati did not capture the movement in the way that Cory Aquino did over a decade ago in the Philippines poses problems in the long term. In many ways a quick political revolution in which Suharto was replaced by someone like Megawati might have prevented a process whereby demands for political and economic change increasingly merge. That is now under way in Indonesia. Democracy and *reformasi* were held up as the solution to millions of people. But these slogans have taken on a life of their own for millions of workers, and urban and rural poor.

The Islamic movement is also split. The most high profile figure is Amien Rais who publicly supported the student protests when it appeared they might succeed in toppling Suharto. Rais's Muhammadiyah organisation claims 28 million members. But Rais welcomed the appointment of Habibie as Suharto's successor claiming Habibie was a good Muslim and was a personal friend. Rais had been purged from the leadership of Indonesia's official Islamic movement by Suharto but was reappointed by Habibie. In early August Rais stated he would be prepared to run for the presidency. But immediately afterwards thousands of people in East Java, many armed with knives, sticks and iron chains, blocked a planned visit by Rais to the city of Surabaya. 'We are ready to kill Amien Rais if he dares enter Pasuran. We need food, not politics', declared one student leader from an Islamic religious school who was blocking a road in Pasuran, 40 miles south of Surabaya.[11]

Many on the left will see Suharto's departure as representing the fall of just another dictator—comparable to Marcos in the Philippines or Duvalier in Haiti. Others will recall that in the 1970s in Spain, after 50 years of fascism, Spanish capitalism was able successfully to make the transition to bourgeois democracy following Franco's death—despite the fact that many on the far left had ruled out that possibility. But the crisis in Indonesia takes place against an economic crisis which in terms of its depth is nearer to that of the 1930s. The replacement of Suharto by Habibie helped diffuse the protests in the short term. But in the medium to long term the presence of Habibie and the continuing rule of the ABRI can generate wider instability.

The demand that Suharto is put on trial and that the wealth he and his family accumulated should be confiscated is very popular.

On a wider level any attempt to disentangle the ABRI from the administration of the country will confront the fact that the armed forces control large segments of the economy. The US and the liberal middle class agree that the ABRI should adopt a simple military role. But achieving that will not be easy. All of this means that fresh protests can quickly radicalise. The student protests acted as the detonator for the revolt of the urban poor. That revolt terrified the ruling class. Working class struggle is developing less spectacularly but it is growing both in militancy and in scale. And there is no absolute gap between the working class and the urban poor. Many workers have found themselves socially marginalised by the economic crisis. The urban poor are not homogeneous. Sections of them can be attracted to ideas like those of Islamic fundamentalism or to anti-Chinese racism. But the working class is in a very strong position to forge real unity. In the meantime a process of polarisation and debate is likely within the universities.

The liberal bourgeoisie and the middle classes talk as if bourgeois democracy can solve the economic crisis, and to many the corruption and nepotism of the Suharto clan was a powerful factor in causing that crisis. But even if Indonesia could move to a form of parliamentary democracy it would do nothing to staunch an economic crisis which is growing in scale across the region. The Indonesian bourgeoisie clearly know that a recession in Japan carries serious implications for Indonesia. Small groups of socialists, often originating from Marxist discussion groups, have the possibility of shifting to mass agitation in the workplaces, among the urban poor and in the campuses. That will require political clarity, professional organisation and the creation of a revolutionary press. The coup in 1965 broke the continuity of Indonesian working class organisation. The most powerful effect of the May 1998 revolution would be to reawaken the heroic tradition of the Indonesian working class and to create a fresh generation of revolutionaries.

Notes

1 *Business Day*, 5 August 1998.
2 *The Indonesian Observer*, 5 August 1998.
3 *Jakarta Post*, 5 August 1998.
4 *Forbes*, 6 July 1998.
5 *The Indonesian Observer*, 5 August 1998.
6 *Jakarta Post*, 18 May 1998.
7 *Jakarta Post*, 22 May 1998.
8 *Jakarta Post*, 5 August 1998.
9 *Jakarta Post*, 5 August 1998.
10 *Jakarta Post*, 22 May 1998.
11 *The Indonesian Observer*, 5 August 1998.

The Algebra of Revolution
The Dialectic and the Classical Marxist Tradition
by JOHN REES

'John Rees has produced a challenging and readable account of the elusive concept of the dialectic. In so doing, he does much to illuminate both the Marxist tradition and the contradictions of contemporary capitalism' —**DAVID MCLELLAN, author of *Karl Marx* and *The Young Hegelians and Karl Marx***

'This is a lively, well-informed, and accessible work on Marxism, which always stays in touch with the historical and social conditions in which theory developed. Rees demonstrates that philosophical issues constantly arise in the revolutionary struggle. Particularly valuable is his discussion of Lukacs. In a word Rees vindicates dialectic as truly the algebra of revolution. Recommended' —**CHRIS ARTHUR, author of *The Dialectic of Labour***

'*The Algebra of Revolution* offers a fresh and superbly clarifying account of the major developments in classical Marxism. It presents this account in terms that a wide range of readers will be able to understand—but with a depth of analysis and reference that will make the book indispensable for advanced students and scholars as well' —**WILLIAM KEACH, Professor of English, Brown University, Providence, USA**

'*The Algebra of Revolution* recaptures the philosophical thread that runs through classical Marxism, and restates and extends this dialectical thought with great clarity and force. It is a work that seeks to restore the continuity of the revolutionary tradition that was broken by Stalin and Hitler, and to make available some of its most creative ideas to a new generation' —**ALEX CALLINICOS, Professor of Politics, University of York and author of *The Revolutionary Ideas of Karl Marx***

'It is without doubt a *tour de force*. Its outstanding characteristic is its exceptional lucidity—the way in which it deals with what are by any standards difficult theoretical issues without oversimplification but with superb clarity' —**JOHN MOLYNEUX, author of *The Future Socialist Society***

Special offer £10.95 (normal price £14.99) available only through Bookmarks, the socialist bookshop, 1 Bloomsbury Street, London WC1B 3QE. Phone 0171 637 1848, fax 0171 637 3416. email bookmarks_bookshop@compuserve.com

Revolution and counter-revolution: lessons for Indonesia

TONY CLIFF

The outbreak of the revolution in Indonesia raises a number of crucial theoretical questions. What are the preconditions for a victorious conclusion to the revolution? In the balance between revolution and counter-revolution, what determines which will triumph? What is the relation between the revolutionary party and the working class? What role does the revolutionary party play in the trade unions? What attitude should the working class take towards the capitalist class and the bourgeois intelligentsia? This article seeks to bring the experience of the Marxist tradition to bear on these crucial questions.

Preconditions for a victorious outcome of the revolution

As Lenin repeatedly stated, we live in the epoch of wars and revolutions. History has proved him right. During the present century more than 100 wars, large and small, have broken out. To mention but a few, chosen at random: the First and Second World Wars, Japan's aggression against China, Italy's war on Abyssinia, the eight year war between Iran and Iraq, US imperialism's attacks on Iraq and Vietnam, the three Arab-Israeli wars, the two India-Pakistan wars, the Falklands War. But many revolutions have also taken place. Again, to mention only some of them: the Russian revolutions of 1905 and 1917, Germany 1918-1923, Spain 1936, Hungary in 1919 and 1956, China 1925-1927, the Portuguese Revolution of 1974, the overthrow of the Shah of Iran in 1979.

What is the nature of a workers' revolution? It is when the mass of workers break from the routine of being victims and passive objects of oppression and exploitation and enter the arena of history, striving to achieve their freedom and shape their destiny. The revolution is not a one day affair. The workers, with new emotions and ideas, still carry with them the baggage of the past. In Marx's words, 'The tradition of dead generations hangs like a nightmare on the mind of the living.' The contradiction at the heart of the revolution is between the new and the old, and only through a very difficult and rigorous process can this contradiction be overcome.

Let us look at some examples, the first being the Russian Revolution of 1917. On 18 February 1917 workers in the largest factory in Petrograd, the Putilov factory where 30,000 workers worked, went on strike demanding a 50 percent wage rise. Bread riots broke out because of the food scarcity. Bakeries and foodstores were stormed, a scene repeated again and again in the following days:

On 23 February at 9am the workers of the plants and factories of Vyborg district went on strike in protest against the shortage of black bread in bakeries and groceries; the strike spread to some plants located in the Petrograd, Rozhdestvenskii, and Liteinyi districts, and in the course of the day 50 industrial enterprises ceased working, with 87,534 men going on strike.

The following day the workers' movement had not abated. Thus a memorandum from the secret police, the *Okhrana*, compiled later in the evening of 24 February, stated:

'The strike of the workers which took place yesterday in connection with the shortage of bread continued today; in the course of the day 131 enterprises with 158,583 workers shut down.'

Next day, on 25 February, the **Okhrana** report expressed even greater alarm, pointing out that troops, and even Cossacks, were not ready to suppress the workers. On 26 February, for the first time, there appears in an **Okhrana** report a direct description of a soldiers' mutiny.

According to N N Sukhanov, an honest eyewitness and excellent chronicler of the revolution, some 25,000 soldiers had left their barracks to mingle with the crowd while the rest of the garrison—altogether 160,000 strong—were not prepared to actually suppress the workers. According to another source as many as 70,000 soldiers joined the 385,000 workers on strike on 27 February.

28 February brought the final collapse of the Tsarist forces: the last remaining 'loyal' troops surrendered; the fortress of Peter and Paul capitulated without firing a single shot; and the Tsar's ministers were either

arrested or else surrendered to the new authorities.

The revolution was completely spontaneous and unplanned. As Trotsky correctly states: 'No one, positively no one—we can assert this categorically upon the basis of all the data—then thought that 23 February was to mark the beginning of a decisive drive against absolutism.'

Sukhanov observes: 'Not one party was preparing for the great upheaval.'

Similarly a former director of the Okhrana stated that the revolution was 'a purely spontaneous phenomenon, and not at all the fruit of party agitation'.[1]

A new political power rose in Petrograd: the soviet. As a matter of fact it was the renewal of an institution that was born in the 1905 Revolution. It was made up of delegates of all workers in the factories on strike, but it went beyond being a unified strike committee. In 1906 Lenin, in retrospect, said the following about the soviet:

*Soviets of Workers' Deputies are **organs of direct mass struggle**. They originated as organs of the **strike** struggle. By force of circumstances they very quickly became the organs of the **general revolutionary** struggle against the government. The course of events and the transition from a strike to an uprising **irresistably** transformed them **into organs of an uprising**.*

The February 1917 Revolution created an exciting new situation: the Tsar abdicated; centuries of the monarchy ended. The police were disbanded. In every factory workers' committees were established. In many army units soldiers' committees came into being. Soviets of workers and soldiers arose everywhere. Already during the 1905 Revolution Trotsky, Chairman of the Petrograd Soviet, could write of these institutions:

The soviet really was a workers' government in embryo... The soviet was, from the start, the organisation of the proletariat, and its aim was the struggle for revolutionary power... With the soviet we have the first appearance of democratic power in modern Russian history... It constitutes authentic democracy, without a lower and an upper chamber, without a professional bureaucracy, but with the voters' right to recall their deputies at any moment. Through its members—deputies directly elected by the workers—the soviet exercises direct leadership over all social manifestations of the proletariat as a whole and of its individual groups, organises its actions and provides them with a slogan and a banner.[2]

But, after the revolution in February 1917, parallel to the soviets, the old institutions continued. In the factories the old owners and the old managers continued to hold to their positions. In the army the generals were still in command: the Commander in Chief of the army was

General Kornilov who was appointed by the Tsar. Parallel to soviet power was a bourgeois government headed by a liberal politician from Tsarist times. This situation, which Lenin and Trotsky called 'dual power', was full of contradictions.

Notwithstanding the nature of the soviet as outlined by Trotsky above, its leaders begged the bourgeoisie to retain power. The majority of the soviet delegates were right wing socialists, Mensheviks and Social Revolutionaries. Out of 1,500 to 1,600 delegates only 40 were Bolsheviks. This was not an accident. It was the inevitable outcome of a situation in which millions of people moved to the left but still carried a lot of the ideological baggage of a Tsarist past. For millions who had hitherto supported the Tsar and the war, a move to the left did not mean straight away joining the most extreme of the parties, the Bolsheviks. The strong man of the Mensheviks, I G Tseretelli, who became Minister of the Interior in the bourgeois Provisional Government, explained the necessity of a compromise with the bourgeoisie: 'There can be no other road for the revolution. It's true that we have all the power, and that the government would go if we lifted a finger, but that would mean disaster for the revolution.'

In a pamphlet entitled *The Tasks of the Proletariat in our Revolution*, Lenin wrote the following on dual power:

This dual power is evident in the existence of **two governments***: one is the main, the real, the actual government of the bourgeoisie, the 'Provisional Government' of Lvov and Co, which holds in its hands all the organs of power; the other is a supplementary and parallel government, a 'controlling' government in the shape of the Petrograd Soviet of Workers' and Soldiers' Deputies, which holds no organs of state power, but directly rests on the support of an obvious and indisputable majority of the people, on the armed workers and soldiers.*

This unstable set-up could not last long:

The dual power merely expresses a **transitional** *phase in the revolution's development, when it has gone farther than the ordinary bourgeois democratic revolution,* **but has not yet reached a** *'pure' dictatorship of the proletariat and the peasantry.*

It was only after days, weeks and months of stormy events that the Bolsheviks managed to win over the majority of workers. On 9 September the Petrograd Soviet went over to Bolshevism and Trotsky was elected as its president. On the same day the Bolsheviks won the majority of the Moscow Soviet. From this point it was only a small stride towards the attainment of workers' power on 7 November 1917.

The May 1968 events in France tell a completely different story with a different outcome. France in May-June 1968 was in a deep social and political crisis. On the night of 10-11 May bloody clashes took place in the Latin quarter of Paris between revolutionary students and the riot police, the CRS. Thousands of young workers joined the students. The next day the CGT, the main trade union federation, called for a protest demonstration. One million people turned up to the demonstration. The unions called for a one day general strike on 13 May and 10 million came out, four times more than the number of workers organised in trade unions. The whole country was paralysed. The CGT and Communist Party leaders hoped that the one day strike and demonstration would serve as an effective safety valve—that this would be the end of the struggle. But they did not reckon with the rank and file, who entered the arena on their own account.

On 14 May the workers of Sud Aviation in Nantes declared an unlimited strike. They occupied the factory and imprisoned the manager in his office. *L'Humanité,* the Communist Party newspaper, tried to ignore the event giving it only seven lines on page 9. The next day the strike and occupation movement spread to all Renault factories. In their footsteps all the engineering factories, the car and aeroplane plants, went on strike and were occupied by the workers. On 19 May the trams stopped along with mail and telegraph services. The subway and bus services in Paris followed suit. The strike hit the mines, shipping, Air France and so on.

On 20 May the strike became a general strike. Some 10 million workers were now on strike. People who had never struck before were involved—Folies Bergère dancers, soccer players, journalists, saleswomen, technicians. Red flags fluttered from all places of work. Not a tricolour was to be seen, notwithstanding the statement of the CGT and CP leaders that, 'Our banner is both the tricolour and the Red Flag'.[3]

All this was very new, representing the future, but the old, 'the tradition of the dead generations', was still hanging on. It is true that 1 million people demonstrated in Paris on 15 May. This was new. But the union bureaucracy, frightened of the thought that the revolutionary students would mingle with the workers, insisted on separating the two groups by creating a cordon of 20,000 stewards holding arms to separate them. It is true that 10 million workers went on strike...*but* the strike committees were not elected but appointed by the trade union bureaucracy. It is true that millions of workers occupied the factories...*but* right from the beginning of the occupations the union bureaucracy insisted that only a small minority of the workers should stay in the factories while the majority were sent home. If all the workers had remained in the occupation the strike would have been active. Now it was passive.

Tragically there was not in existence a large revolutionary organisation that could overcome the bureaucracy. In Russia in March 1917 the Bolshevik Party had 23,600 members and this number increased by August to 250,000. The French industrial working class was significantly larger than the Russian working class in 1917. Had there existed a revolutionary organisation of some tens of thousands, it could have argued that the workers' contingents in the demonstration should not be separated from the students. It could have called for democratic elections of strike committees and could have convinced the millions occupying the factories to remain inside the factories, creating a collective force many times stronger than when these same workers were simply an aggregation of individuals. Alas, the total number of revolutionaries in France could be counted in hundreds.

Therefore, it was not long before the government got the unions to agree to a compromise with the employers on a wage rise. The occupation of the factories ended, the strike was called off, and the ground was prepared for the return of the president, General de Gaulle. When the factories were occupied de Gaulle was so demoralised that he had flown out of the country to find refuge with the French troops in West Germany. But now he came back to rule once more. On 30 May a right wing demonstration of half a million people took place in Paris. The police seized back the TV and radio stations, threw out occupying workers, attacked any continuing demonstrations and even killed two workers and a school student. Again and again during 1968 the revolutionary potential, which could have gone so far, stopped well short of victory. And this has been the pattern in other revolutions.

In November 1918 the revolution in Germany got rid of the Kaiser and brought the First World War to an end. Alas, big employers like Krupps and Thyssen remained along with the generals and the reactionary army officers who set up right wing units called *Freikorps*. As in Russia, dual power prevailed in Germany, for side by side with parliament were the workers' councils. Under the umbrella of the Social Democratic government, *Freikorps* officers murdered revolutionary leaders Rosa Luxemburg and Karl Liebknecht. The revolutionary events continued with ups and downs until 1923, but they ended with the victory of capitalism. The Nazi movement was born in 1919. In 1923 it organised a 'failed' coup in Bavaria, but it was waiting in the wings. This was another lost opportunity for workers and they would pay for it dearly when Hitler came to power.

France in the 1930s saw a massive rise of working class struggle which started in February 1934 and culminated in 1936 in a decisive victory of the Popular Front—an alliance of the Communist Party, Socialist Party and Liberals (who were mistakenly called Radical

Socialists—they were neither radical nor socialist). Millions of workers said to themselves, 'Now we own the government, let's take over the factories.' And in June 1936 a wave of factory occupations took place. The leaders of the Communist Party and Socialist Party, however, led a retreat following a compromise with the employers. After this the CP was thrown out of the Popular Front. It was the Radical Socialist Daladier who signed the Munich agreement with Hitler in 1938, and it was the same parliament elected in the great Popular Front victory of 1936 which voted support for Marshal Pétain, head of the Vichy regime which collaborated with the Nazis from 1940 onwards.

The Middle East is another area which has seen great upheavals which shook the establishment but failed to win a fundamental breakthrough. In Iraq, King Feisal was overthrown in 1951 by a mass movement. The Communist Party of Iraq was a very strong party, indeed the strongest CP in the Arab world. It entered into an alliance with the bourgeois nationalist party, the Ba'ath. The Communist Party, under Stalinist control, believed that the coming revolution would be a democratic one, which demanded an alliance between the working class and the bourgeois parties. Such an alliance means in practice the subordination of the former to the latter. The Communist Party members and the workers paid a heavy price for this alliance. The Ba'ath, headed by General Saddam Hussein, with the aid of the CIA, carried out a mass slaughter of Communists.

In Iran a general strike led to the overthrow of the Shah in 1979. *Shoras* (workers' councils) mushroomed throughout the country. Tragically the leadership of these *shoras*, largely the pro-Moscow Tudeh Party and the Fedayeen, saw the revolution as a bourgeois democratic revolution instead of a proletarian one, and so gave support to the establishment of the Islamic republic. Ayatollah Khomeini thus came to power without showing any gratitude to the Tudeh or Fedayeen, and the left was subjected to bloody repression.

All the above events completely confirm the prophetic words of St Just, a leader of the French Revolution of 1789: 'Those who half make a revolution dig their own grave.' To complete the revolution and bring it to full victory, the proletariat has to be led by a revolutionary party. The working class, not the party, makes the revolution, but the party guides the working class. As Trotsky aptly wrote:

> *Without a guiding organisation the energy of the masses would dissipate like steam not enclosed in a piston box. But nevertheless what moves things is not the piston or the box, but the steam.*[4]

The difference between success and failure, between Russia in

October 1917 and all these other examples, was that in the former case there was a mass revolutionary party providing effective leadership. While socialists cannot determine the moment when the revolutionary crisis breaks, they do determine the eventual outcome by the degree to which they build a strong revolutionary party.

The revolutionary party and the working class

The heart of Marxism is that the emancipation of the working class is the act of the working class. *The Communist Manifesto* states:

> All previous historical movements were movements of minorities, or in the interest of minorities. The proletarian movement is the self-conscious, independent movement of the immense majority, in the interest of the immense majority.

At the same time the *Manifesto* also stresses: 'The ruling ideas of each age have ever been the ideas of its ruling class.' There is a contradiction between the two statements. But the contradiction is not in Marx and Engels' heads. It exists in reality. If only one of the statements were correct, the victory of the working class would either be inevitable or impossible. If the workers were not imbued with capitalist ideas—selfishness, apathy towards other workers, racism, sexism, etc—socialism would be inevitable. It would come into being even if revolutionaries did not lift a finger. If workers completely accepted the ideas of the ruling classs, socialism would be impossible and this would remain so forever. The balance between the two factors—self activity of the working class and subordination to ruling class ideas—is not static. It changes all the time. Sometimes the changes can be slow and imperceptible over a long period, but then they can change dramatically in a very short time.

The sharpening of the class struggle which leads to increasing confidence among workers undermines the hold of bourgeois ideas. Conversely, a downturn in workers' combativity following serious, continuous defeats, or mass unemployment over a long period (that erodes the self confidence of the workers), makes them more ready to imbibe reactionary ideas.

However, a change in the balance between the two factors does not depend only on what happens in the workplace, on the economic front. Engels wrote that the class struggle takes place in three fields: the economic, the political and the ideological. The three fields are of course interconnected, with the economic serving as the base and the political and ideological as the superstructure. But workers' combativity can rise, and even explode, not only because they are victorious in a struggle over wages or against sackings, but also because of events in the political field.

The Russian Revolution of February 1917 was not the result of a big rise in strikes, but was a direct reaction to the war. Four million Russian soldiers had perished. Hunger stalked the country. The riots and demonstrations in Petrograd at the beginning of February ignited the revolution, but these events had very little connection with a rise in the level of the industrial struggle.

The balance between the two factors—the new thinking that grows out of self activity of workers and the burden of capitalist ideas—does not alter only with changes in the general situation, but also affects different workers differently. One can say that in any given situation one section of workers completely accept bourgeois ideas—these are the conservative workers. Another section completely rejects bourgeois ideas—they are the revolutionary workers. Those two groups are represented by two separate parties—a conservative party and a revolutionary workers' party. Between these two there is another group of workers on whom a third type of workers' party is based—the reformist party. One example of such a party is the British Labour Party. In a speech to the Second Congress of the Communist International in 1920, Lenin defined the Labour Party as a 'capitalist workers' party'. He called it capitalist because its politics did not break with capitalism. Why did he call it a workers' party? It is not because the workers voted for it. At that time more workers voted for the Conservative Party and this party was purely a capitalist party. Lenin called the Labour Party a workers' party because it reflected the urge of workers to defend themselves against capitalism.

Of course this is a very rough classification. Between the revolutionary parties and the reformist parties there can also be another kind of party—the centrist party. Its main characteristic is fudge and vacillation. It is neither one thing nor another. A centrist party sometimes moves from the right to the left, or from the left to the right. And the same centrist party can change direction over a very short space of time. The centrist party is like a chameleon, changing its colour but never remaining consistent.

A great danger for a revolutionary party is that it adapts itself to the centrists while in turn the centrist party tail-ends the reformists and the latter tail-ends the capitalist party. To give just one example: during the general strike of 1926 in Britain the leadership of the Communist Party softened and adapted their key policies, hoping by this method to attract the centrist trade union leaders. As a result they tail-ended the likes of A J Cook, George Hicks and Alfred Purcell, the left leaders of the general council of the TUC. For their part Cook, Hicks and Purcell tail-ended the right wing leadership of the TUC—Jimmy Thomas, Arthur Pugh and Ben Turner. These three followed the leadership of Ramsay MacDonald, leader of the Labour Party, and ended up effectively supporting the policy of Stanley Baldwin, the Conservative prime minister of the day. The Communist Party's adaptation to the centrists led finally to a terrible defeat of the British working class. A revolutionary party facing vacillating centrist leaders must demonstrate clarity and steadfastness; one has to be firm to steady the unsteady.

History is made by the working class and so the revolutionary party must avoid two dangers: the first is substitutionism, believing that the party can act for the class; the second is opportunism, adapting itself to views prevailing in the class. To give an example: a revolutionary can stand on a picket line, and find next to them a worker who makes racist comments. The revolutionary can do one of three things: say, 'I'm not standing with a racist on a picket line. I'm going home.' That is sectarianism, because if the emancipation of the working class is the act of the working class, one must side with the workers against the employers, however backward the individual worker. Another possibility is to avoid facing up to racism. When the worker makes a racist comment, one can pretend one hasn't heard, and say, 'The weather's quite nice today, isn't it?' This is opportunism. A third possibility is to argue with this person against racism. If they are convinced, excellent, if not, still, when the strike breakers come, one links arms, because the emancipation of the working class *is* the act of the working class. A revolutionary cannot afford either substitutionism or tail-ending the workers.

A successful revolution also depends on the revolutionary party acting as the university of the working class. The situation of the working class vis-à-vis the bourgeoisie is radically different to the position of the early bourgeoisie when it was in rebellion against the feudal lords. The capitalists, even when their class was very young, were intellectually independent of the nobility. It is true the capitalists had to overthrow the nobility, as the working class today has to overthrow the capitalists. But the working class lacks the advantages enjoyed by the bourgeoisie when it sought to make a revolution. Its enemy, the nobility, did not own all the wealth as do the capitalists today. As a matter of fact, the nobility were not as rich as the capitalists. The capitalist could turn round to the nobility and say, 'All right, you own the land, but we own money, we own the banks. When you go bankrupt how do you try to save yourself? You try to mix your blue blood with my gold. You try to marry my daughter.' When it came to the intellectual battle, the capitalist could turn round and say, 'Alright, you have the church, but we have the university, you have priests but we have professors; you have the Bible, but we have the encyclopaedia. Come on, move over.'

The capitalists influenced the nobility much more than the nobility influenced the capitalists. The French Revolution started with a meeting of Estates General (the Three Estates—the nobility, the priesthood and the middle classes). When it came to the vote many nobles and priests voted with the capitalists, not the other way round. Is the position of the workers today vis-à-vis the capitalists similar to this? Of course not. The workers cannot turn round to the capitalists and say, 'All right, you own Fords, General Motors, ICI, etc. We own...' In terms of ideas there are hardly any capitalists influenced by the socialist press, while there are millions of workers influenced by capitalist propaganda.

When we say that the revolutionary party is the university of the working class, it means we have to learn from the historical and international experience of the working class, both its triumphs as well as its defeats. The revolutionary party must be the memory of the working class. Thus in looking at Indonesia today one must also bear in mind the experience of the first workers' government in the world, the Paris Commune of 1871, where workers held power for 74 days. We have to learn from the 1905 Revolution, and even more so from the victory of the October Revolution. At the same time we have to learn from the defeat of the German Revolution of 1918-1923; from the defeat of the general strike in Britain in 1926; from the murder by Stalin of all the leaders of the Bolshevik Party after Lenin's death, his annihilation of the soviets, and his replacement of the proletarian regime which stood for the beginning of socialism with a state capitalist order. One has to learn from the 1933 catastrophe in Germany, when the strongest, best organised workers' movement in the world capitulated to the Nazis without a fight, because it was led by two parties one of which was a right wing reformist party and the other a Stalinist party. One has to learn why in China society has developed in such a way that there are at the top a massive number of millionaires, while at the bottom there are hundreds of millions who live in abject poverty.

To give confidence to workers' struggle, the revolutionary party must have theoretical clarity. Its converse, theoretical scepticism, is incompatible with revolutionary action. As Lenin said, 'The important thing is to be confident that the path chosen is the right one, this confidence multiplying a hundredfold revolutionary energy and revolutionary enthusiasm, which can perform miracles'.[5] Without understanding the laws of historical development, one cannot maintain a persistent struggle. During the years of toil and disappointment, isolation and suffering, revolutionaries cannot survive without the conviction that their actions fit the requirements of historical advance. In order not to get lost on the twists and turns of the long road, one must stand firm ideologically. Theoretical scepticism and revolutionary relentlessness are not compatible. Lenin's strength was that he always related theory to the processes of human development. He judged the importance of every theoretical notion in relation to practical needs. Likewise he tested every practical step for its fit with Marxist theory. He combined theory and practice to perfection.

Lenin believed in improvisation. But in order for this not to degenerate into simply the shifting impressions of the day, it had to be blended into a *general perspective* based on well thought out theory. Practice without theory must lead to uncertainty and errors. On the other hand, to study Marxism apart from the struggle is to divorce it from its mainspring—action—and to create useless bookworms. Practice is clarified by revolutionary theory, and theory is verified by practice. The Marxist traditions are assimilated in the minds and blood of women and men only by struggle.

Building a revolutionary party

By far the greatest Marxist in his understanding of the role of the revolutionary party and its activity was Lenin. His experience in building the Bolshevik Party from 1903 onwards is very instructive. The embryo of the revolutionary party is the discussion group, the study circle. This is a necessary stage in the 'primitive accumulation of cadres'. But it is only a stage. The circle mentality has serious weaknesses. It is amateurish and can become an impediment to the development of a revolutionary party proper.

In 1902 in a brilliant pamphlet entitled *What is to be Done?* Lenin argued that the Russian revolutionaries had to put an end to the circle mentality. The revolutionaries, he argued, had to build a centralised, all-Russian organisation. To achieve this they had first of all to fight against what he called *Kustarichestvo*—a primitive 'handicraft method of organisation'. They had to establish a strong organisation made up of professional revolutionaries; this was especially needed under the illegal, harsh conditions of Tsarism. But to prevent the organisation becoming a sect it had to establish strong ties with workers and their struggles. The key to this is the party paper. The paper must serve as a weapon for building a centralised all-Russian organisation. In an article called 'Where to Begin' he wrote that 'the role of a newspaper' should not be:

> ...limited solely to the dissemination of ideas, to political education, and to the enlistment of political allies. A newspaper is not only a collective propagandist and a collective agitator, it is also a collective organiser. In this last respect it may be likened to the scaffolding round a building under construction, which marks the contours of the structure and facilitates communication between the builders, enabling them to distribute the work and to view the common results

achieved by their organised labour. With the aid of the newspaper, and through it, a permanent organisation will naturally take shape that will engage, not only in local activities, but in regular general work, and will train its members to follow political events carefully, appraise their significance and their effect on the various strata of the population, and develop effective means for the revolutionary party to influence those events. The mere technical task of regularly supplying the newspaper with copy and of promoting regular distribution will necessitate a network of local agents of the united party, who will maintain constant contact with one another, know the general state of affairs, get accustomed to performing regularly their detailed functions in the all-Russian work, and test their strength in the organisation of various revolutionary actions.

This network of agents will form the skeleton of precisely the kind of organisation we need—one that is sufficiently broad and many-sided to effect a strict and detailed division of labour; sufficiently well tempered to be able to conduct steadily **its own work** *under any circumstances, at all 'sudden turns', and in face of all contingencies; sufficiently flexible to be able, on the one hand, to avoid an open battle against an overwhelming enemy, when the enemy has concentrated all his forces at one spot, and yet, on the other, to take advantage of his unwieldiness and to attack him when and where he least expects it.*[6]

The party paper is *the organiser of the party.*
But with the outbreak of the 1905 Revolution Lenin changed his argument: *the party should not be made up of professional revolutionaries but be based on mass recruitment.* In the spring of 1905, at the Russian party congress, Lenin proposed a resolution urging the party to open its gates wide to workers, who should be brought forward to take a leading role in it. The party should:

...make every effort to strengthen the ties between the party and the masses of the working class by raising still wider sections of proletarians and semi-proletarians to full [revolutionary socialist] *consciousness, by developing their revolutionary...activity, by seeing to it that the greatest possible number of workers capable of leading the movement and the party organisations be advanced from among the mass of the working class to membership of the local centres and of the all-party centre through the creation of a maximum number of working class organisations adhering to our party, by seeing to it that working class organisations unwilling or unable to enter the party should at least be associated with it.*[7]

In an article called 'The Reorganisation of the Party', written in November 1905, Lenin says bluntly, 'The working class is instinctively, spontaneously' revolutionary socialist.[8] As a result of this reorientation the party membership exploded. While in 1903 the membership was counted in hundreds, in October 1906 the Bolshevik Party had some 33,000 members.[9] Without Lenin's understanding that the development of the party requires very different tactics and forms of organisation tailored according to the size of the organisation, the composition of its membership, and the tasks required of it by the balance of forces in the wider society, such growth would not have been possible.

The revolutionary party and the trade unions

Revolutionaries are involved in every aspect of workers' struggle. Hence they are deeply involved in the struggle of the trade unions. The reformists regard the working class movement as split into different, separate compartments: economic struggle, that is the task of the trade unions; politics, ie participation in parliamentary and local government elections, is the concern of the reformist parties. Against this the Marxist looks at the working class as a totality, as a class that uses two arms in the struggle—the economic and the political.

In general the dichotomy between economic and political struggle is foreign to Marx. An economic demand, if it is sectional, is defined as 'economic' in Marx's terms. But if the same demand is made of the state it is 'political':

> The attempt in a particular factory or even in a particular trade to force a shorter working day out of individual capitalists by strikes, etc, is a purely economic movement. On the other hand the movement to force through an eight-hour, etc, **law**, is a **political** movement, that is to say, a movement of the **class**, with the object of enforcing its interests in a general form, in a form possessing general, socially coercive force...every movement in which the working class comes out as a **class** against the ruling classes and tries to coerce them by pressure from without is a political movement.[10]

In many cases economic (sectional) struggles do not give rise to political (class wide) struggles, but there is no absolute separation between the two, and many economic struggles *do* spill over into political ones. The experience of Russia in 1905, with mass strikes acting as the motor of revolution, gave new depth to the understanding of the close connection between the economic and political struggles. Rosa Luxemburg pointed out that in a revolutionary period the economic struggle grows into a political one, and vice versa:

> The movement does not go only in one direction, from an economic to a political struggle, but also in the opposite direction. Every important political

mass action, after reaching its peak, results in a series of economic mass strikes. And this rule applies not only to the individual mass strike, but to the revolution as a whole. With the spread, clarification and intensification of the political struggle not only does the economic struggle not recede, but on the contrary it spreads and at the same time becomes more organised and intensified. There exists a reciprocal influence between the two struggles. Every fresh attack and victory of the political struggle has a powerful impact on the economic struggle, because as it widens the scope for the workers to improve their conditions and strengthens their impulse to do so, it enhances their fighting spirit. After every soaring wave of political action, there remains a fertile sediment from which sprout a thousand economic struggles. And the reverse also applies.

The logical and necessary climax of the mass strike is the 'open uprising which can only be realised as the culmination of a series of partial uprisings which prepare the ground, and therefore are liable to end for a time in what look like the partial "defeats", each of which may seem to be "premature".' And what a rise in class consciousness results from the mass strikes!

The most precious thing, because it is the most enduring, in the sharp ebb and flow of the revolutionary wave, is the proletariat's spiritual growth. The advance by leaps and bounds of the intellectual stature of the proletariat affords an inviolable guarantee of its further progress in the inevitable economic and political struggles ahead.[11]

It would be a great mistake to conclude from the above that there is no important qualitative difference between the party and the unions. This is especially important for countries like Indonesia in which the unions are just at the beginning of their existence and the border between the two is quite often very unclear. The slogan of the unions was set down in Britain in the 19th century: 'A fair day's pay for a fair day's work.' The aim of the revolutionaries, the socialists, is to abolish the wages system, to get rid of a society in which some people have to sell their labour power and others buy it. Obviously so long as capitalism exists we prefer high wages to low ones but the different goals remain.

The unions recruit members on a radically different basis to the revolutionary party. The revolutionary party recruits those who are in ideological agreement with its principles. The unions aim to recruit every worker, revolutionary, reformist or conservative. It strengthens the unions if conservative workers are involved and under the ideological pressure of all other workers. The revolutionary party, by contrast, should not dilute its membership by including people who do not agree with its politics. The trade union movement is a blunt axe but a large one.

The revolutionary party is a sharp axe even if it is relatively small. Lenin contrasted the roles of the revolutionary Marxist with the trade union secretary:

> For the secretary of any, say English, trade union always helps the workers to carry on the economic struggle, he helps them to expose factory abuses, explains the injustice of the laws and of measures that hamper the freedom to strike and to picket (ie to warn all and sundry that a strike is proceeding at a certain factory), explains the partiality of arbitration court judges who belong to the bourgeois classes, etc, etc. In a word every trade union secretary conducts and helps to conduct 'the economic struggle against the employers and the government'...the Social Democrat's ideal should not be the trade union secretary, but the **tribune of the people**, who is able to react to every manifestation of tyranny and oppression, no matter where it appears, no matter what stratum or class of the people it affects; who is able to generalise all these manifestations and produce a single picture of police violence and capitalist exploitation; who is able to take advantage of every event, however small, in order to set forth **before all** his socialist convictions and his democratic demands, in order to clarify for **all** and everyone the world-historic significance of the struggle for the emancipation of the proletariat.[12]

The revolutionary party and the liberal factions in the democratic revolution

In a whole number of countries where the bourgeoisie is young and the political regime is either autocratic or only recently became democratic, such as Indonesia, there is a danger that the proletariat will tail the bourgeois democrats. The French bourgeoisie succeeded in carrying out their revolution of 1789-1793, but since then the pattern has been different. For example, the German bourgeoisie of 1848 betrayed their revolution and capitulated to the landowning *Junkers* and the monarchy. The German bourgeoisie was fearful of the rising working class. Today the working class exists everywhere and is employed in much larger plants than existed in 1789 or 1848. Fear of the proletariat inevitably paralyses the bourgeoisie and the bourgeois intelligentsia. In March 1850 Marx argued that the German working class should not subordinate itself to the liberal bourgeoisie and petty bourgeois intelligentsia:

> The relation of the revolutionary workers' party to the petty-bourgeois democrats is this: it marches together with them against the faction which it aims at overthrowing, it opposes them in everything by which they seek to consolidate their position in their own interests.
>
> Far from desiring to transform the whole of society for the revolutionary proletarians, the democratic petty bourgeois strive for a change in social conditions by means of which the existing society will be made as tolerable

and comfortable as possible for them...

While the democratic petty bourgeois wish to bring the revolution to a conclusion as quickly as possible...it is our interest and our task to make the revolution permanent, until all more or less possessing classes have been forced out of their position of dominance, the proletariat has conquered state power... For us the issue cannot be the alteration of private property but only its annihilation, not the smoothing over of class antagonisms but the abolition of classes, not the improvement of the existing society but the foundation of a new one...

It is self-evident that in the impending bloody conflicts, as in all earlier ones, it is the workers who, in the main, will have to win the victory by their courage, determination and self-sacrifice. As previously so also in this struggle, the mass of the petty bourgeois will as long as possible remain hesitant, undecided and inactive, and then, as soon as the issue has been decided, will seize the victory for themselves, will call upon the workers to maintain tranquillity and return to their work, will guard against so-called excesses and bar the proletariat from the fruits of victory...they themselves must do the utmost for their final victory by making it clear to themselves what their class interests are, by taking up their position as an independent party as soon as possible and by not allowing themselves to be misled for a single moment by the hypocritical phrases of the democratic petty bourgeois into refraining from the independent organisation of the party of the proletariat. Their battle cry must be: The Revolution in Permanence.[13]

Some one and a half centuries later the bourgeoisie and bourgeois intelligentsia are even more cowardly and reactionary. The revolutionary party must keep its distance from them, even if they take on a reddish coloration. The most prominent leaders in Indonesia today are Megawati and Amien Rais. Megawati is the daughter of the first president of Indonesia, Ahmed Sukarno. When Indonesia won its independence from the Dutch in 1949 the country was led by this bourgeois nationalist. His ideology was based on the principles of *pancasila* whose main planks were belief in god and national unity. Tragically the Indonesian Communist Party did not challenge Sukarno, but, on the contrary, agreed with him completely on the need for national unity. The result was that St Just's words came true: 'Those who make a half revolution dig their own graves.'

The Communist Party of Indonesia had far more members than the Bolshevik Party had at the time of the revolution: 3 million as against a quarter of a million. The working class of Indonesia was larger than the working class of Russia on the eve of the revolution. The peasantry was larger in Indonesia than in Russia. In 1965 a general appointed by Sukarno, one Suharto, organised a coup with the backing of the United States, the British Labour government and Australia. Somewhere between half a million and a million people were slaughtered. Megawati has not advanced one inch further than her father.

The other most prominent leader of bourgeois nationalism in Indonesia at present is Amien Rais. He does not stand to the left of Megawati. He is the chairman of the Muslim movement, *Muhammadiya*, which claims 28 million members. He has for years been engaged in the most disgusting racist agitation against the Chinese minority in Indonesia, which led to pogroms on a massive scale, the main victims of which were the very poor. Amien Rais was harsh on the Chinese, but quite accommodating to President Suharto. On 19 May, two days before Suharto's abdication, Amien Rais appeared on radio and television calling on people not to demonstrate, to keep calm!

Megawati and Amien Rais are pygmies compared to Robespierre or Danton and in no way more militant than the cowardly bourgeoisie in Germany in 1848 that Marx so sharply castigated.

Indonesia, like many Third World countries, faces serious bourgeois democratic tasks—achieving political democracy, solving the agrarian question, overcoming the fragmentation of the country, and putting an end to the oppression of national and religious minorities as well as to the oppression of women and gays. Only after the proletariat achieves a victorious revolution can these democratic tasks be fully carried out. At the same time in the struggle for workers' power the revolutionary party must act as a tribune of the oppressed and mobilise the energy of the peasants, the national and religious minorities, women and gays.

Notes

1 T Cliff, *Lenin*, vol 2 (London, 1976) pp76-82.
2 L Trotsky, *1905* (New York, 1972) pp251, 253-254.
3 C Harman, *The Fire Last Time, 1968 and After* (London, 1998) pp2-6.
4 L Trotsky, *History of the Russian Revolution* (London, 1997) p19.
5 V Lenin, *Collected Works*, vol IX (Moscow, 4th edn) p103.
6 V Lenin, *Collected Works*, vol VII, p363.
7 V Lenin, *Collected Works*, vol VIII, pp409-410.
8 V Lenin, *Collected Works*, vol X, p334.
9 T Cliff, *Lenin*, vol I (London, 1975) p179.
10 K Marx, F Engels, V Lenin, *Anarchism and Anarcho-Syndicalism* (Moscow, 1972) p57.
11 T Cliff, *Rosa Luxemburg* (London, 1983) pp35-36.
12 V Lenin, *Collected Works*, vol V, p423.
13 K Marx and F Engels, *Collected Works*, vol X (London, 1981) pp280-282, 287.

The legitimacy of modern art

JOHN MOLYNEUX

The attempt to produce a socialist or Marxist response to contemporary visual art or to any particular examples of it, such as to Damien Hirst, to the 'Sensation' exhibition or to the Turner Prize, runs immediately into the problem of the legitimacy, or rather the lack of legitimacy, of modern art. This is the fact that much, if not all, of modern art (painting, sculpture and similar visual production since around 1900) is regarded as a dubious or perhaps downright fraudulent activity by a substantial proportion of at least four groups of people: (1) the general public, ie the working class; (2) the tabloid press and related media journalists (newscasters, current affairs pundits, etc); (3) a section of the 'educated/cultural' middle class; (4) the philistine bourgeoisie proper. The result is that the history of modern art is punctuated by numerous 'art scandals' in which sections of the press, the media and the public either get upset or pretend to get upset about the latest artistic 'outrage', be it Jackson 'Jack-the Dripper' Pollock or Carl André's 'bricks' (*Equivalent VIII*) or Marcus Harvey's *Myra*. It is also that the media response to every new development in modern art is almost invariably conducted under the repetitive rubric of 'Is it art?'

Art academics and art world professionals seldom address the 'Is it art?' question. On the one hand they have such a strong vested interest in the answer that even raising the question is seen as bad form—a concession to philistinism. On the other hand their tendency to talk only to each other within their ivory towers enables them to cheerfully disregard what most 'ordinary' people think of as a matter of little consequence. For

Marxists, however, the consciousness of the working class is a matter of vital importance. Precisely because we regard the working class as the agent of its own emancipation, what workers think—about politics above all, but also about religion, philosophy, culture etc—does count. We fight to raise the consciousness of the class, to expand its horizons, to develop its individual and collective personalities. If many or most workers are influenced by philistine prejudices regarding modern art or art in general this damages their personalities and, albeit indirectly, their struggle. It is therefore our duty to combat those prejudices.[1] On the other hand, Marxists' opposition to bourgeois ideology as a whole and scepticism about passing intellectual and academic fads—genetic determinism and postmodernism, for example—ensures that we cannot simply take it for granted that what the director of the Tate Gallery tells us is good art must be so. The 'Is it art?' question is therefore a real question and not one whose answer can be simply assumed in advance. Moreover a historical materialist approach suggests that the fact of widespread hostility to modern art has itself to be interrogated and explained with the anticipation that such an enquiry will tell us something significant about the position of art in our society.

The peculiarity of modern art

The crisis of legitimacy I am talking about has applied at one time or another to all the arts in the 20th century—to the poetry of T S Eliot and Ezra Pound, the novels of James Joyce, the plays of Samuel Beckett, the music of Schoenberg and so on. However, it is also clear that the crisis is most severe, ie the scepticism is most extreme, widespread and long lasting, in relation to visual art. The television panel discussion of the Booker Prize in 1997 criticised the shortlist and denounced the winner; it did not attack the modern novel as such. The television debate on the Turner Prize, however, even though plainly designed to promote the prize and the Tate Gallery, felt obliged to include two individuals—Janet Daley and Roger Scruton—deeply antagonistic to much of contemporary art. What explains this state of affairs?

The first factor is clearly the nature of the modernist transformation of painting and sculpture as compared with that experienced by other art forms such as music and literature. It was both more rapid and more radical. In 1907 Picasso painted *Les Desmoiselles D'Avignon*. In retrospect we can see that the painting had many antecedents.[2] Nevertheless it constituted a dramatic break with the 500 year old tradition of oil painting initiated by the early Renaissance at the very dawn of the bourgeois era. This break had several aspects to it: (1) the drastic foreshortening of the picture plane and thus the abandonment of the practice, pioneered by Uccello, Mantegna and others in the 15th century, of creating an illusion of three dimensional perspective and depth within the picture frame; (2) an abandonment of the even older tradition, initiated by Cimabue, Giotto and Masaccio, of three dimensional 'plastic' modelling of figures through light and shade, in favour of slabs of flat surface; (3) an abrupt discarding of the techniques so painstakingly acquired by artists such as Van Eyck and Holbein, Titian and Rubens, of precise naturalistic rendering of furs, silks, laces, flesh tones, metals, glass and numerous other surfaces; (4) a sharp assault, especially, but not only, through the use of African masks, on the norms of female beauty embodied in virtually every representation of the female nude from Botticelli's *Venus* to Renoir.

So shocking was *Les Demoiselles D'Avignon* that it offended even Picasso's avant-garde artist friends and remained face to the wall in his studio, unexhibited until 1937.[3] However, the painting opened the way to, or, in John Berger's phrase, 'provoked', Cubism[4] which passed rapidly through its analytic and synthetic phases.[5] In the footsteps of Cubism came Futurism, Vorticism, Rayonism, Suprematism, Dadaism and abstract art. Within ten years of *Les Desmoiselles* we have both Duchamp's *Fountain*[6] and Malevich's *White Square on White*. Add another six or seven years and we have also Constructivism, De Stijl (including the emergence of Mondrian's trademark style) and Surrealism. Thus in the space of little more than a decade, visual art goes through such a revolution that painters and sculptors are producing work which would simply have been unrecognisable as art in any previous period. The gap between the painting of Constable and Turner on the one hand and that of Mondrian, Pollock or Rothko on the other, or between the sculpture of Rodin and the three dimensional work of Duchamp, Beuys or Robert Smithson is much wider than the gap between the music of Beethoven or Tchaikovsky and the music of Schoenberg or Birtwistle, or the gap between Dickens and Joyce or Keats and Ginsberg.[7] The first factor explaining the extremism of this modernisation is clearly the invention of photography (and even more so of cinema, television and video) which deprived visual art of what, for centuries, had been one of its principal functions—the naturalistic representation of the appearance of persons and things.[8] Prior to the mid-19th century the only way in which the likeness of an individual or his/her clothes and possessions, or a visual image of Jesus or Mary, or the appearance of a palace or garden, or civic ceremony, could be recorded for posterity or made available to people unable to see them with their own eyes was through the art of the painter, sculptor, engraver etc. Suddenly, in historical terms, the camera placed the ability to achieve a more or less exact likeness in the hands of millions of people at minimal cost and with minimal skill. No other art form suffered a comparable mechanical usurpation of its core function and skills and consequently no other art form was compelled to reorient itself so radically.

Another factor involved was a socio-political shift in regard to the representation of the ruling class that took place in the first half of the 19th century. As John Berger showed in his *Ways of Seeing*, the main subject matter of European oil painting—its daily bread and butter from the 15th century onwards—has been the ruling classes and their possessions (clothes, land, horses, wives, mistresses, children, etc). Somewhere between the Great French Revolution and the revolutions of 1848 there is a change both within the ruling class itself and within the stratum of the middle class that produces most artists. On the one hand, the rich and powerful become coy. Gradually they lose the desire to be visibly personally glorified—perhaps it makes them feel too exposed as tempting objects of expropriation. It shows in their clothes and it changes their attitude to art.[9] Rockefeller, Getty, Guggenheim and Saatchi want the reflected glory of owning great art collections but they do not seem interested in hagiographic portraits of themselves. Similarly the artists lose interest in painting the ruling classes. The result is that David's *Napoleon* is probably the last important painting glorifying a ruler.[10] Goya painted the Spanish royal family, of course, but with devastating satire; Géricault painted inmates of the local mental asylum; Manet painted the prostitute 'Olympia', the barmaid at the Folies Bergère, and only the *execution* of the Emperor Maximilian, and Van Gogh painted peasants and postmen.

Art, deprived of one of its main social functions and of much of its traditional subject matter, transformed itself almost beyond recognition and in so doing lost much of the cultural credit it had accumulated over centuries. However, this is not the only factor involved in modern art's special crisis of legitimacy. There is also the peculiar way in which the art market works that is distinct from the operation of the literary market or the music market or the cultural market generally. Despite the hopes and expectations of Walter Benjamin, the art market, and with it the art world, is dominated by the individual or institutional ownership of individual 'unique' works of art. This has a series of complex effects on the nature of the art world and on the production and consumption of contemporary art. Art works are surprisingly expensive to produce, requiring costly materials, studio and other storage space and exhibition space. This is true of the traditional oil painting, especially if it is large. It is even more true of sculpture and current installation work—Damien Hirst's 'Shark'[11] is rumoured to have cost £80,000 to construct.[12] They are even more expensive to buy. Anyone who thinks a ticket for Covent Garden is extortionate should try buying a work of art. Not a famous 'old master' (which rarely come on the market and fetch millions when they do); not a Matisse or a Picasso (which range from many millions for the major works to about £250,000 for some offhand piece); not a Pollock, a Rothko or a Lichtenstein (also probably over the million mark) but a painting by a contemporary British artist with something of a national reputation, say a Calum Innes or a Gary Hume, both runners up in previous Turner Prize competitions. You are still looking at around £10,000—ie a price completely out of reach of all but the spectacularly rich.

One consequence of this is that both the art market and the art world are dominated by an extraordinarily small number of rich and powerful individuals—a few immensely wealthy collectors and patrons, of whom Charles Saatchi is currently the most important in Britain, and the managers of a few key institutions, such as the Tate Gallery in London or the Museum of Modern Art and the Whitney Museum in New York. The other significant players are those big corporations who decide to invest in art such as the Japanese company that paid over £27 million for a Van Gogh *Sunflowers*[13] and state institutions and local authorities who have significant commissions in their gift. For Marxists it is a truism that under capitalism the bourgeoisie dominates culture but in visual art the elitism is much more pronounced than in other art forms. In neither literature nor music could one individual buy themselves influence comparable to that wielded by Saatchi today or by Peggy Guggenheim in the 1950s, and Alfred Barr Jr at MOMA in the 1930s and 1940s. In other art forms, with the exception of the special case of architecture,[14] the logic of the market links financial reward with some degree of mass popularity such as numbers of books or records sold, numbers of seats sold for performances etc, while both rewards and popularity are distinct from critical acclaim. In painting and sculpture mass popularity is almost irrelevant; both financial and critical success depend on appealing to the tiny elite of art world makers and shakers.

Thus while there is a general working class and petty bourgeois antagonism to so called high culture, it is more intense in the sphere of visual art. This is particularly the case because the *artistic* value of paintings and sculptures is always posed by the media *and* the art world in terms of their *monetary* value. No one asks how much *Hamlet* or *The Waste Land* or Beethoven's Fifth Symphony are 'worth'; the question is absurd. Yet it is precisely this question that always comes to the fore with works of visual art and it cannot fail to arouse public resentment. In a world where hunger and poverty, homelessness and unemployment are rife, it is both inevitable and right that 'ordinary' people object to spending millions or hundreds of thousands on works of art that serve no obvious practical function. When the money spent is public money and the art it is spent on seems incomprehensible (because of the modernisation process discussed earlier) the objections are likely to be fierce. The question of money pollutes the art world and undermines its public legitimacy.

Another factor in modern art's crisis of legitimacy, which is both a consequence and cause of public alienation from art, is the virtual absence of what might be called popular art culture. When we speak of high culture and popular culture in relation to literature, it is clear that on the one hand there is the literary canon, old and new, from Chaucer to Beckett as it were, and on the other hand, there are popular writers from Agatha Christie to Jeffery Archer. There are also innumerable figures who sit somewhere in the spectrum between high and low—Kipling and Tolkien, Le Carré and Walsh. Also between the highbrow literary novelist and poet and pulp fiction there lie several sub-genres—science fiction, the spy novel, the whodunit etc, each with a passionate popular following and each capable of producing work of some literary merit. In music the vibrancy of the popular is even more pronounced. Between Mahler and the Spice Girls stands everything from Gilbert and Sullivan to jazz and flamenco.[15] In art there is no equivalent. There are illustrators, cartoonists, Sunday painters and painters of animals and Jade ladies for sale in Woolworths but no one, including the people who buy this stuff, takes any great interest in it as art, or holds it in high esteem. High modern art therefore stands in a kind of splendid isolation with no buffer between it and public scepticism.

This analysis, hopefully both historical and material, shows that the legitimacy crisis of modern art is neither an accident nor a conspiracy but a historically conditioned phenomenon produced by the combination of the loss of its long standing practical functions and its economically positioned elitism and isolation.[16] It is an analysis which is a necessary preliminary to answering the 'Is it art?' question but is not in itself an answer to it, and it is to this question that we must now turn.

But is it art?

How one answers or tries to answer this question/objection depends on what one takes it to mean. It can be interpreted in a number of different ways. First it can be a claim that some/much/all modern art is a deliberate confidence trick. Second it can be taken absolutely literally as a claim that some/much/all 'modern art' is misnamed because it lacks the characteristics necessary for it to qualify as art. Third it can be a claim that whether or not it technically qualifies as art it is more or less worthless because it lacks skill. Fourth it can be that the problem with modern art is that it is difficult, too difficult for 'ordinary' people to understand. Let us explore each of these interpretations of the question.

It has to be acknowledged straight away that fraud, deception, confidence trickery, in the strict legal senses of these terms not only exist in the world of visual art but are much more common here than in any other art form. There are certainly hundreds, probably thousands, of fake Picassos, Matisses, Monets, Mirós etc, swimming around in the art market and adorning the walls of the rich, and not a few hanging in major collections. There are two obvious reasons for this. The first is the nature of the art market that I have discussed already—its focus on the ownership of individual unique objects. The second is the still dominant cult of the individual artistic genius, which makes the monetary, and to an extent the critical, 'value' of an artwork the product of the 'genius' and not its merits as a painting or sculpture.[17]

Nevertheless, the idea that modern art as a whole or even predominantly is a confidence trick clearly doesn't stand up. After all, who is supposed to be tricking whom? If it is meant to be the artists tricking the public then the exercise is a conspicuous failure: most of the public have remained resolutely unfooled and most of the artists fail to make any money. If the artists are tricking the rich patrons then not only does this suggest remarkable naivety on the part of the Rockefellers, Gettys and Saatchis but also raises the question of how they manage to do so well out of being conned. Anyone 'conned' into buying Pollock or Rothko, Lichtenstein or Warhol, must have cursed all the way to the bank.

But if modern art is not a conscious and deliberate deception this does not mean it cannot be a collective delusion. Perhaps, just as millions of people believe in gods which don't exist, and millions believed that Russia was socialist when it wasn't, other millions or thousands have fallen for the illusion that strange, meaningless objects are works of art. However, the problem with saying that certain objects are not art is that it implies a clear definition or conception of what art is. If an explorer or a naturalist comes across a new creature they can usually establish if it is a mammal because there is a generally agreed and quite precise definition of what constitutes a mammal, reptile, bird etc.[18] Does such a definition exist for 'art'?

Certainly not in the minds of most journalists and members of the public who protest that Damien Hirst's shark or Carl André's bricks or whatever are not art. Rather what exist in their minds tend to be assumptions or prejudices which have not been subject to critical examination and in fact will not stand up to such examination. For example, there is a quite common assumption that art should involve naturalistic representation or 'imitation' of objects in the real world. However, apply this criterion rigorously and look what gets excluded and included. 'Out' would be not only a lot of Picasso, Braque, Mondrian, Pollock, Miró, Moore and Brancusi, but also African art, Muslim art, Australian

Aboriginal art and even Giotto. 'In' would be not only Constable, Turner, Holbein, Van Eyck and Velázquez but also the Sunday paintings of Winston Churchill and Prince Charles and, ironically, the ready-mades of Marcel Duchamp, the screen prints of Warhol and Hirst's pickled animals. Moreover there is the problem of music, one of the three fundamental art forms and undoubtedly the most popular, which is hardly at all about the representation or imitation of 'reality'. If it is acceptable for a composer or musician to use an arrangement of notes to express and communicate emotions, why should not an artist like Kandinsky or Rothko use an arrangement of colours and forms for the same purpose?

There are many other such assumptions that are more or less widely held: that art should be 'beautiful' or 'pretty'—'as pretty as a picture';[19] that paintings should be made of oils or watercolours and sculpture of stone or bronze, not other materials; that paintings should employ single point perspective. On investigation most of these assumptions turn out simply to be superficial generalisations drawn from the established practice of European art from about 1400 to 1900.

However, probably the most commonly aired objection to modern art is that it lacks 'skill'—that 'my four year old child could do that', as it is often put. This charge needs quite careful discussion because modern art is so variable in this respect. On the one hand, there are many modern artists where the claim that they lack skill can be made only on the basis of ignorance. Picasso is an obvious example. A child prodigy, he was exceptionally skilled in traditional representational painting in his teens. By his early twenties (the 'Blue Period', 1901-1904) he had already produced naturalistic work that would earn him a significant place in art history. His Analytical Cubist works such as *Seated Nude* of 1910 in the Tate Gallery or *Man with a Guitar* of 1911 in the Paris Musée Picasso are paintings of profound technical skill and Picasso retained an astounding technical facility throughout his life. Then there is the case of Jackson Pollock. Pollock also began as a figurative and Social Realist artist in the 1930s arriving at his characteristic Abstract Expressionist or action painting only in 1947-1948. In these works Pollock gave up easel painting with brushes in favour of dripping and flicking paint from a stick onto huge canvases laid out on the floor. At first glance these paintings could be dismissed as a chaotic mess, a product of random spraying of the paint, lacking all control or skill—but only at first glance. Closer inspection of individual works, comparison of one work with another, and viewing of the famous film of Pollock at work all confirm that the artist had achieved a very high level of control of the drip technique and that each painting has a very definite and specific overall effect. Pollock's skill is not the same as Dürer's in rendering the fur of a hare or Titian's in painting red hair but it is still skill in the handling of paint.

On the other hand there are modern artists who clearly involve skill in their work but it is not skill in handling paint or carving stone, modelling clay or casting bronze. Take for example, Rachel Whiteread, winner of the Turner Prize in 1993, who makes casts (usually in plaster) of the insides of domestic objects ranging from hot water bottles and baths to rooms and a whole house. To make a cast of the inside of a room or a house strikes me as a really difficult thing to do. I certainly would have no idea how to begin doing it and I imagine that innumerable technical problems would crop up on the way. Can you control the outcome? How do you get the cast out? How do you move it? How do you store it? And so on. But, of course, the skills involved are not those conventionally associated with art. The same applies to an artist using video such as the Palestinian exile Mona Hatoum. To make *Corps Étranger*, Hatoum used an endoscope to film the passages inside her body and then projected the resulting video onto the floor within a cylindrical structure which the viewer has to enter to see the work. Once again all sorts of technical skills are involved but not traditional art skills.

Finally there are a very small number of cases where the element of technical or craft skill deployed is so small as to be effectively non-existent. The most extreme examples are the ready-mades of Marcel Duchamp—*Bottle Rack* (1914), *Bicycle Wheel* (1913) and the afore-mentioned *Fountain* (1917)[20]—and the brick sculptures of Carl André—*Lever* (1966) which consists of 137 firebricks laid side by side across the floor in a single row at right angles to the wall and *Equivalent I-VIII* (1966) which consists of eight permutations of a basic unit of 120 sand-lime bricks laid on the floor of a single gallery.[21] To many people the absence of craft skills in these works is proof that they cannot be art. But in fact, André's bricks and Duchamp's ready-mades retain one crucial skill that they share with Hatoum and Whiteread, Pollock and Picasso, and, indeed, with Michelangelo: the intellectual skill to conceive of the work. This intellectual skill may have several different elements: the understanding or perhaps intuition (and, indeed, courage) to see that a pile of bricks or whatever could be moving or beautiful; the aesthetic skill to arrange the bricks etc in a form that would be moving or beautiful;[22] the intellectual under-standing of art, art history, society etc to conceive how a particular intervention such as exhibiting a urinal or line of bricks could make a meaningful point or raise significant questions.[23] This argument does not establish that these works are 'good' or 'important' art but it does answer the claim that they are not art of any sort because they are 'only' a bottle rack or bricks.

So far I have been considering and rejecting the arguments and assumptions underpinning the 'Is it art?' approach of the media etc. But is it not possible to find within the realms of the art world and art theory or else to construct a positive definition of art that can enable us, in principle at least, to decide these questions?

The definition of art

There are many in the art world who would either deny the possibility of producing a definition of art or, even more damningly, proclaim that it was not an interesting question. Significantly Peter and Linda Murray's *Dictionary of Art and Artists* (Penguin, 1973) contains definitions of everything from Action Painting to Vorticism but no entry for 'art' as such, while Charles Harrison and Paul Wood's monumental *Art in Theory* (1900-1990), which contains over 300 extracts of writing on art from Cézanne to Serra, includes only one text which addresses the task of defining art. This denial is disingenuous. In practice art world people whether they are artists, dealers, curators or critics make distinctions all the time between art works and non-art works.[24] Consequently the failure to establish a definition of art means that the criteria on which these distinctions are made remain unarticulated and unexamined.

In so far as any definition does have currency in the art world it is that 'art is whatever artists do' or more precisely 'art is what artists do and call art' (since no one claims that *every* action by an artist is art). This is also, as far as I can see, the 'real' position of most of those who purport to reject the question. It is a definition which has arisen out of the experience of modern art with its constant innovations and transformations and particularly in response to the practice of Duchamp and his successors. In appearance this definition is radical and open, able to cope with and accept all new developments. In reality, however, it is a deeply conservative and elitist position—indeed it embodies the elitism of the art world already referred to. If art is what artists do, what makes someone an artist? The obvious answer that an artist is someone who makes art is ruled out because it renders the first definition circular. This leaves only two possible replies: that some special individuals are born artists (which is akin to the doctrine that the ruling classes are born to rule), or that artists are those people whom the art world, ie its dominant institutions, recognises as artists. This definition therefore is a case of self validation by a self-perpetuating elite.[25]

If this definition must be rejected it nevertheless has the merit of not attempting a definition in terms of common qualities inhering in the art works. Such an attempt will fail because of the enormous heterogeneity of such objects, because artists have and will set about transgressing any imposed limits, and because art has a generic meaning covering a wide variety of forms of creative practice (music, poetry, drama, etc) which do not produce commensurable 'objects' but nonetheless have a clear social affinity. The element of truth in the 'art is what artists do' definition is that it points in the direction of the nature of artistic labour. This can be followed up in a Marxist way using the approach developed by Marx for the analysis of capital and commodities.

Marx insisted that while capital could take the form of machinery or money neither machinery nor money were capital as such. They only became capital within certain social relations of production:

> A negro is a negro. He only becomes a slave in certain relations. A cotton spinning jenny is a machine for spinning cotton. It becomes capital only in certain relations.[26]

Equally the products of human labour are not in themselves commodities. They become commodities only in the context of the social relation that is the market. The analysis of the commodity requires, therefore, the analysis of that social relation and, in particular, of the nature of the human labour that produces the commodity and underlies the market relation:

> Whence, then, arises the enigmatical character of the product of labour, so soon as it assumes the form of commodities? Clearly from this form itself...
>
> A commodity is therefore a mysterious thing, simply because in it the social character of men's labour appears to them as an objective character stamped upon the product of that labour: because the relation of the producers to the sum total of their own labour is presented to them as a social relation, existing not between themselves but between the products of their labour...
>
> This fetishism of commodities has its origin, as the foregoing analysis has already shown, in the peculiar social character of the labour that produces them.[27]

If we apply this approach to art we can say that paint or other marks on a flat surface, arrangements of words on paper, sequences of sounds in the air etc, only became art in certain social relations. The question 'What is art?' then becomes, what is the peculiar social character of the labour that produces what we call art? The answer to this question is that 'art' is the product of *non-alienated* labour.

This is clearly a contentious and contested claim and I cannot enter a full defence of it here.[28] I will restrict myself to a few comments of clarification and justification. By non-alienated labour I do not mean labour that exists 'outside' of capitalism (which is increasingly non-existent), or labour that does not produce commodities (the massive commodification of art under capitalism is obvious), or even labour that people enjoy (some people 'enjoy' some alienated labour and some non-alienated labour is not enjoyable).[29] Still less do I mean that 'artists' are not alienated or that their work does not reflect and express alienation—alienation affects everyone in capitalist society. What I mean is labour that remains under the control and direction of the producer.

According to Marx in the *1844 Manuscripts* the essence of alienated labour lies in the relationship of the worker to his/her work, to the productive activity itself:

> *Thus, when we ask what is the important relationship of labour, we are concerned with the relationship of the worker to production.*
>
> *So far we have considered the alienation of the worker only from one aspect: namely, his relationship with the products of his labour. However, alienation appears not merely in the result but also in the process of production within productive activity itself. How could the worker stand in an alien relationship to the product of his activity if he did not alienate himself in the act of production itself?...*
>
> *What constitutes the alienation of labour? First, that the work is external to the worker, that it is not part of his nature; and that, consequently, he does not fulfil himself in his work but denies himself, has a feeling of misery rather than well-being, does not develop freely his mental and physical energies but is physically exhausted and mentally debased. The worker, therefore, feels himself at home only during his leisure time, whereas at work he feels homeless. His work is not voluntary but imposed, forced labour. It is not the satisfaction of a need, but only a means for satisfying other needs. Its alien character is clearly shown by the fact that as soon as there is no physical or other compulsion it is avoided like the plague. External labour, labour in which man alienates himself, is a labour of self-sacrifice, of mortification. Finally, the external character of work for the worker is shown by the fact that it is not his own work but work for someone else, that in work he does not belong to himself but to another person.*[30]

Artistic labour differs from this in that, even when the work is to fulfil a commission or to produce a commodity to be sold, the productive activity itself remains the possession of the artist and in that work he/she belongs to herself, not to another person. In contrast to alienated labour, artistic labour is a development and expression, not a denial and distortion of the producer's physical and mental energies. It requires money to sustain it but it is not simply a means of earning money.

The very young Marx expressed this idea in the context of defending the freedom of the press in 1842:

> *A writer must of course earn a living to exist and be able to write, but he must*

in no sense exist and write so as to earn a living. When Beranger sings: 'I only live to make my songs. If you rob me of my place, Monsignor, I will make songs in order to live.' There is an ironic avowal in this threat: the poet falls from his domain as soon as his poetry becomes but a means. In no sense does the writer regard his works as a means. They are **ends in themselves**.[31]

The much older Marx makes the same point in the context of discussing productive labour in *Theories of Surplus Value*:

Milton produced **Paradise Lost** *for the same reason that silkworms produce silk. It was an activity of his nature. Later he sold the product for £5. But the literary proletarian of Leipzig who fabricates books (for example,* **Compendia of Economics**) *under the direction of his publisher is a productive labourer; for his product is from the outset subsumed under capital and comes into being only for the purpose of increasing that capital.*[32]

Trotsky is, I believe, expressing the same underlying idea, though in less precise, less scientific language, when he writes that 'spiritual creativeness demands freedom'[33] and, 'Art is basically a function of the nerves and demands complete sincerity',[34] and, 'Art, like science, not only does not seek orders, but by its very essence, cannot tolerate them'[35] —propositions on which he bases his insistence that the revolutionary party should not aspire to command art either before or after the conquest of power.

There are two obvious objections to the argument made so far. The first is that many works of art are in fact made with large amounts of alienated, wage labour, for example films. The second is that many works of non-alienated labour are not art, for example Lenin's *State and Revolution* or do-it-yourself work around the house.

My answer to the first objection is that most works of art involve a combination of alienated and non-alienated labour: think of the quarry workers who cut Michelangelo's marble, the session musicians at a recording, the paper makers, typesetters and printers necessary for the poet's slim volume and so on. However, it is the non-alienated labour that gives the work its artistic character. The poetry book is not possible without the labour of the printer but it is the labour of poet that makes the slim volume 'art', while the telephone directory is not art. The same applies to films, concerts, plays, operas, architecture etc and all those collective art forms that make extensive use of alienated labour from extras and ushers, to ticket collectors and building workers. In each case what makes them art is the non-alienated labour contributed by directors, composers, soloists, designers, architects etc.[36]

The second objection is clearly valid in its own terms. I would meet it by acknowledging that only a particular kind of non-alienated labour produces art, namely labour in which there is a unity of form and content or, to be more precise, where the form *is* the content. Lenin's writing of *The State and Revolution* was undoubtedly unalienated labour but it was labour in which the content—the exposition and development of the Marxist theory of the state—far outweighed in significance the form— the specific words employed to convey the meaning. *State and Revolution* in English or in French is essentially the same work as in the Russian original, provided the translation is competent nothing fundamental is lost. It is quite otherwise with the poetry of Mayakovsky. A translation of a poem is not at all the same as the original because in poetry the exact words count: the meaning of a poem consists not merely of the sum total of the dictionary definitions of the words used but also of all those words' connotations, their sounds and their rhythm. When Mr Smith builds for himself a garden wall it is again unalienated labour but the exact form of the wall is secondary to its practical function— making an effective division between Mr Smith's garden and Mr Jones's, or whatever. But when Carl André forms 960 bricks into *Equivalent I-VIII* there is no practical function but the shape, colour and precise positioning of every brick is what makes it the work it is.[37]

This analysis of art as unalienated labour that unites form and content solves a number of problems. First, it resolves the paradox that on the one hand art is evidently a historically universal activity more or less coextensive with the history of the human species; while on the other hand, 'art' as a separate activity and especially 'artist' as a recognised social role emerge and become distinct only from the Renaissance onwards. Of course, human beings have always engaged in non-alienated labour, making music, painting pictures, carving wood etc, but it is only with the rise of capitalism and the concomitant intensification of alienated labour that art and therefore the artist become sharply differentiated from and counterposed to ordinary social labour.

Second, it enables us to understand Marx's statement that 'capitalist production is hostile to certain branches of spiritual production, for example, art and poetry'.[38] Clearly there is a serious problem in trying to argue that the bourgeoisie as a class is hostile to art. From the Medicis to the Saatchis, from Mrs and Mrs Andrews to Nelson Rockefeller, sections of the bourgeoisie have patronised art and basked in its reflected glory. Moreover capitalist states and governments have generally shown a fairly keen awareness of the significance of art for their overall ideological hegemony. Nor can it plausibly be claimed that the bourgeois epoch has been artistically impoverished compared to the feudal epoch nor other epochs in history. But Marx speaks neither of the bourgeoisie nor the bourgeois epoch but of capitalist production. Capitalist production is production on the basis of alienated labour. In so far as artistic production becomes incorporated within capitalist production, in so far as capital assumes complete control over the process of production of art, that production ceases to be artistic and ceases to produce art. When Orson Welles made *Citizen Kane* he made a work of art; when he made a sherry commercial, he did not.[39] It is this *objective* antagonism between unalienated and alienated labour that lies at the root of the *subjective* antagonism of artists towards capital and capitalism, which is a recurring trope in the bourgeois epoch and not just a romantic or bohemian myth.

This definition also makes it possible to resolve in summary and fairly sweeping fashion the whole repetitive 'Is it art?' debate. The answer is yes. Whether it is Malevich's *White Square on White*, Pollock's *One 1950*, Whiteread's *House* or Hirst's *Mother and Child Divided*, it is all art because it all meets the criteria of unalienated labour striving for unity of form and content. This does not, however, make it good or great art, which is a different question.

Is modern art difficult?

Before turning directly to the relative merits of modern and contemporary art I want to discuss a claim often made about modern art which has important implications for its legitimacy; namely, that it is 'difficult'. Interestingly this claim is made both by critics and defenders of modern art. On the one hand it is said that understanding modern art requires specialist knowledge and study and this makes it elitist and inaccessible to the masses. Art, it is argued, *ought to* communicate with 'ordinary' or 'working class' people. On the other hand it is argued that the best modern art is indeed difficult but it is precisely its difficulty that makes it good. It is not the fault of modern art that it is difficult or that the masses are insufficiently educated to understand it: it has to be difficult in order to deal with complex challenging issues and to advance art. There are also right wing and left wing variants of both these arguments. There is a right wing populism exemplified by the tabloids which denounces the 'intellectualism' of modern art as part of its general attack on the 'liberal' intelligentsia. There is a left populism, often espoused by the Communist Parties in the 1930s, which demands art—usually naturalist art—accessible to the workers. There is a right wing elitism that views the masses as more or less congenitally incapable of scaling the sublime heights of great art and a left elitism which attributes the indifference of the masses towards art to their cultural impoverishment by class society and capitalism.[40]

In so far as these as the categories exhaust the options, I would place myself in the 'left elitist' camp with Luxemburg and Trotsky but I want to challenge the assumption that modern art is in some special way difficult. The question is quite complicated because works of art can be 'difficult' in different ways. Difficulty can be culturally relative. To someone who reads only English a novel in French is impossibly 'difficult' even if it is written by Barbara Cartland. This kind of difficulty is one of the factors making Chaucer or Shakespeare 'difficult' for modern readers. Similar to this is what we might call the 'difficulty of the new'. T S Eliot observes that 'difficulty may be due just to novelty: we know the ridicule accorded in turn to Wordsworth, Shelley and Keats, Tennyson and Browning'[41] and certainly contemporary critics found Manet difficult,[42] not to speak of the Impressionists who now seem so easy and natural. Then there is genuine intellectual difficulty in the sense that Hegel's *Logic* and parts of Marx's *Capital* are difficult or theoretical physics is difficult or the difficulty of Eliot's *The Waste Land* with its quotations in half a dozen languages and its references to Ovid, Ecclesiastes, *The Golden Bough*, Dante, the Upanishads and so on. Finally there is the distinction which has to be made in this context between 'understanding' and 'appreciation' which though they may often be linked are not always so and are by no means identical.[43]

With these considerations in mind we can consider the relative 'difficulty' and 'accessibility' of traditional and modern art. In reality much traditional art requires very considerable, and sometimes quite esoteric, knowledge to be understood. Thus most medieval art and much from the early modern period assumes a knowledge of the Bible (or of classical mythology) which is not held by most people today. For example one cannot understand Rembrandt's *Bathsheba*—even in the literal sense of knowing what is being depicted—unless one knows the relevant Bible story. It also makes a significant difference to know that the model for Bathsheba was Heindricke Stoeffels, the woman Rembrandt loved and lived with for the last 20 years of his life, but that knowledge is only available from study. Moreover much art of this period uses a complex iconography, in which particular objects have very specific meanings, knowledge of which has long since passed out of the common culture and is now very much the preserve of specialist scholars. An example of a famous painting whose meaning can only be fully grasped on the basis of a knowledge of its iconography is Hans Holbein's *The Ambassadors* with its disguised 'memento mori' or reminder of death.

In contrast there are many works of modern art that can be appreciated with little or no knowledge or study. As I write I am looking at a reproduction of a painting by Miró called *Blue III*. It is a very simple painting. It consists of a field of blue which covers the whole canvas. Towards the bottom right corner there is a smallish flat black ovoid. Running from near the bottom left corner to near the top right corner is a meandering thin black line, like a piece of string or thread of cotton. At the top of the black line is a small red oval blob. That's it. Now it so happens I know next to nothing about this painting. It was painted in 1961 but other than that I don't know its history. I have not read any theoretical analyses or 'interpretations' of it and cannot offer any interpretation of my own apart from the fairly obvious observations that the blue is suggestive of the sky and the line and red blob of a kite. If the painting has a deeper 'intellectual' meaning, I don't know what it is. And yet looking at this painting gives me great pleasure. It evokes feelings of delight, of playfulness and of the joy of life. I could analyse, at least to some extent, how and why the painting evokes these feelings but the analysis would be secondary. I do not have to do, or be able to do, the analysis to experience the feelings. To avoid misunderstanding I should stress that I am not claiming that my response to *Blue III* is 'pure' or 'innocent' or not socially conditioned or uninfluenced by knowing that Miró is 'famous' or by my general knowledge of art history or anything like that, but *only* that the Miró is not intrinsically more 'difficult' than a Rembrandt or Holbein. Perhaps the most important 'knowledge' I need to enjoy and be moved by the Miró is the knowledge that a non-representational painting can be a valid work of art and can evoke such a response.

Another example is provided by Picasso's *Guernica*. Clearly an understanding of this painting is facilitated and enhanced by the information that it was a response to and protest against the bombing of the historic Basque city in 1937 by the Luftwaffe during the Spanish Civil War and that this was the first instance of aerial bombing of civilians and so on.[44] Nevertheless, it is a fact which I have established through 'experiments' with students that the painting 'speaks' and conveys at least some of its 'meaning' (outrage at the horror and suffering of war) to people who have no knowledge of its specific history. Certainly it conveys its meaning to the non-specialist as effectively as or more effectively than many an acknowledged 'old master'—provided, of course, that the non-specialist concerned is not possessed of the fixed conviction that the 'meaning' of painting consists primarily or solely in naturalistic imitation.[45]

One way in which works of modern art are sometimes said to be 'difficult' is that they are contributions to or interventions in the ongoing 'story of art' and therefore cannot be understood unless one knows the story so far, that is unless one is familiar with the history of art. There is an important element of truth in this in at least two ways: (1) every new modern art movement, every significant new work, exists in dialectical tension with the work that preceded it (Surrealism grows out of the failure of Dadaism, Cubism develops in opposition to Fauvism etc); (2) specific works frequently 'quote' or 'reference' other specific works from the past (for example, Mark Wallinger's horse paintings in the 'Sensation' exhibition reference the horse paintings of George Stubbs in the 18th century). Doubtless it helps to have the knowledge of art history to pick up on these relationships. But this is in no way a characteristic peculiar to either modern or visual art. The history of painting in the Renaissance can be told through successive representations of the Madonna and Child by Cimabue, Giotto, Masaccio, Leonardo, Raphael etc. Manet's *Olympia* references Titian's *Venus of Urbino*, and Seurat's *The Bathers* both develops and challenges Impressionism while echoing the frescos of Piero della Francesca. The poetry of Keats wrestles with the legacy of Milton and Shakespeare and his most famous sonnet is inspired by a 17th century translation of Homer.[46] Even that most popular of cultural forms, post-war pop and rock music, operates and develops in the same way, as does Marxist theory.

But is this trait more prevalent in modern art than in traditional art or other art forms and is it more than just part of what modern art works are doing? If the answer to this is yes, it would make modern art not so much difficult as shallow, superficial and sterile.[47] It would reduce modern art to a series of illustrations of essays in a hermetically sealed art history 'discourse' with nothing significant to say about or to its times. A work of art no matter how much it develops out of or against a tradition must stand in its own right and work visually on its own account if it is to be taken seriously.

I believe the better examples of modern art do precisely this and the evidence I would cite is the relative popularity of modern art. Obviously modern art is not popular in the sense that football or *EastEnders* are popular, but it is popular in the sense of appealing to a substantial constituency of people, a constituency much wider than the art world elite, pretentious bourgeois, or people with expert knowledge. In February of this year I went to a lecture by Christo and Jeanne-Claude (famous for 'wrapping' the Reichstag and the Pont Neuf) at South Downs College just outside Havant. Tickets at £10 a time were sold out well in advance and something like 700 people attended. That is a significant audience. Walk into any bookshop and you will see large numbers of art books including modern art books, many in cheap editions (like the Taschen editions which include Ernst, Grosz, Duchamp, Klee, Miró, Mondrian and Rivera). This is true not only of Dillons, Foyle's and the like, but of The Works which specialises in cheap remaindered books in Portsmouth's central shopping precinct.

Then there is the evidence of gallery and exhibition attendance. Over the last five years (1993-1997) attendance at the Tate Gallery has averaged 1,944,177 per year with a peak of 2,226,399 in 1994. Over a similar period (1992-1996) the Tate Gallery, Liverpool, averaged 534,422 per year and the Tate Gallery, St Ives, averaged 164,046.[48] Interest in modern art is confirmed by attendance at particular exhibitions: over 300,000 at 'Sensation' and 157,754 at 'Braque:The Late Works'—both at the Royal Academy in 1997, compared with only 98,756 at the more traditional Summer Exhibition; at the Tate Gallery 408, 688 for Cézanne in 1996, 296,648 for Picasso in 1994, and 114,275 for Mondrian in 1997, but only 169,412 for Constable in 1991; and at the Hayward Gallery 111,525 for Howard Hodgkin and 'Beyond Reason:Art & Psychosis' in 1996-97, and 101,092 for 'Objects of Desire:The Modern Still Life'.

All in all this amounts to a very considerable audience for modern art, larger, I believe, than the audience for modern poetry[49] or serious modern theatre or contemporary classical music. But what kinds of people make up this audience? According to the Tate Gallery's visitor research they are in terms of age and gender broadly representative of the nation with a slight bias towards women and people under 35. There is also an entirely predictable strong bias towards the middle class—88 percent of visitors are ABC1s and only 11 percent C2DEs when these categories constitute 49 percent and 51 percent respectively of the population. However, by Marxist class criteria C2DEs represent only the manual working class, while a significant proportion of Bs and C1s are white collar workers rather than middle class and in any case these figures suggest at least 100,000 manual workers visiting the Tate Gallery each year—a statistic which certainly gives food for thought.

Finally there is the vague, impressionistic evidence provided by the use of modern art images and styles in mainstream culture—in adverts, music videos, graphics, textiles and everyday design. Persil ran an advertising campaign featuring 'Mrs Picasso's Washing'. Stella Artois had a joke ad, 'Is it art...or is it Artois?' A little while ago there were Mondrian cigarette lighters all over the place and L'Oreal aerosols and sprays were all themed á la Mondrian. The sleeve of *Sergeant Pepper*—perhaps the most popular album of all time—was designed by modern artist Peter Blake. In some ways this is the most important evidence of all—despite its lack of precision—for it shows modern art doing its work affecting, influencing, developing the visual culture, the aesthetics, of the society as a whole. It shows modern art operating on how people see things often without them even knowing it and it confirms in practice what I have argued at various points in this essay: namely that the obstacle to the popular appreciation of modern art is often neither the art itself nor the inherent incapacity of the public but the elitist social ambience and construction of the art world combined with dogmatic but outdated conceptions of what art should look like.

Is art in decline?

I raise this question because even if it is accepted that 'modern art' and indeed current art is genuine art which needs to be taken seriously there is still a quite widespread view that it constitutes a decline from some previous high point or higher plateau. What is more, this is not just a conservative view held by the likes of Roger Scruton or Peter Fuller, it is a position common, perhaps even dominant, among Marxist or Marxist influenced writing on art.

From the outset we should be clear about the considerable care required in formulating this question so that it can be answered meaningfully and the enormous difficulty involved in offering any kind of serious response to it based on empirical judgement. What time scale are we operating on and what are we comparing with what? Are we comparing the art of the 1990s with the art of the 1980s, the 1970s or some previous decade? Or are we comparing the art of the second half of the 20th century with the art of the first half of the century? Or the 20th century with the 19th century or with some other previous century or with all other previous centuries? Are we talking about the art of one country, of Europe, of the so called 'West' or of the world?

There are pitfalls every step of the way. It is obviously unreasonable to compare the art of this year or this decade with the art of a whole century or period in the past. Yet psychologically it is very easy to fall into this and what is more to select as the point of comparison a particularly outstanding period. No, Damien Hirst and the 'Young Brit Art' of today don't match up to Michelangelo or the Quattrocento but how do they compare to, say, Italian painting of the 1890s or British sculpture of the 1790s?[50] The matter is complicated by the fact that different art forms do not develop evenly within particular countries and visual art does not develop evenly across different countries even within Europe. Thus Elizabethan/Jacobean England is an exceptionally rich period in terms of literature (Shakespeare, Marlowe, Jonson, Donne, Webster, Spenser etc) but produces nothing remotely comparable in painting and sculpture. Seventeenth century Holland gives us Rembrandt, Hals, Ruysdael, Vermeer, Hobbema and others in painting but neither literature nor sculpture of world historical importance. In the second half of the 19th century everything really vital and important in visual art seems to be concentrated in France (Courbet, Manet, Monet, Pissarro, Sisley, Renoir, Degas, Cézanne, Seurat, Gauguin, Van Gogh, Redon etc) but this is not true of other art forms—think of Russian literature. Then there is the question of art outside North America and Europe. Who really knows what is happening now or has been happening in the last decade or so in the visual art of Latin America, Africa, the Middle East and South East Asia and who would feel confident to make aesthetic judgements about it all? And if it were possible to pronounce with assurance that the art of the 1980s and 1990s was on a downward curve worldwide from the 1960s and 1970s (or some similar proposition), could one be sure that the trend would continue into the next millenium or is it just about to bottom out? There is also an important cultural/psychological factor which is likely to affect all our judgments. The acknowledged great artists of the past, the Giottos and Raphaels, the Titians and Velázquezes, have been accumulating cultural credit for centuries. For centuries they have been bywords for genius featuring in anecdotes by Vasari, the metaphors of Marx, the aphorisms of Picasso[51] and so on. It is very difficult to rank a contemporary artist still alive, perhaps still young, their work uncompleted, alongside the established giants of the past.

But if it is virtually impossible to produce a sustainable empirical judgement on this question, can it nevertheless be answered theoretically? Is it possible on general theoretical grounds, ie on the basis of a theory of overall historical development, to assert that art is, or is likely to be, or must be undergoing a process of decline? This is a question which seems to sit up and beg for a ready made Marxist answer: art reflects society (in the final analysis); capitalism is a society in crisis and decay (in the final analysis); bourgeois art is therefore decadent and in decline (in the final analysis). To this apparent syllogism it is possible though not mandatory to append the claim that modernism is the expression or epitome of bourgeois decadence.

This, in its crudest, most dogmatic and sectarian form was the position of Stalinism in its Zhdanovite phase and, in infinitely more cultured and sophisticated form, of Lukács who was operating, albeit critically, within the Stalinist camp. However, many Marxists have been drawn by the argument. Here is Plekhanov, writing before modernism really to into its stride:

> *I said and (I would like to think) demonstrated in my lecture that contemporary art was in decline...by the word 'decline' I mean,* **comme de raison**, *the whole process, and not any particular episodes. This process is not yet complete, just as the social process of the collapse of the bourgeois order is not yet complete. It would be strange to think therefore, that present day bourgeois ideologists are utterly incapable of producing any kind of outstanding work at all. It stands to reason that, even at this stage, such works are possible. But the chances of their appearance are being drastically reduced. What is more, even outstanding works bear the imprint of the period of decadence.*[52]

This is Francis Klingender, of the Artists' International Association and author of *Art and the Industrial Revolution*, in 1935:

> The development of modern art from impressionism to abstract form...embodies the ever more frantic flight from content i.e. from social reality, from all reality whatever, of the retrogressive capitalist class... Far from achieving the emancipation of art the destruction of content necessarily leads to the destruction also of form—a climax epically symbolized in the white square painted on a white canvss of square shape by the supremacist Malevich. In its final decay the capitalist class destroys its art as it destroys its science.[53]

And here is Trotsky writing in 1938:

> ...a declining capitalism already finds itself completely incapable of offering the minimum conditions for the development of tendencies in art which correspond, however little, to our epoch. It fears superstitiously every new word, for it is no longer a matter of corrections and reforms for capitalism but of life and death... The artistic schools of the last few decades—Cubism, Futurism, Dadaism, Surrealism—follow each other without reaching a complete development. Art, which is the most complex part of culture, the most sensitive and at the same time the least protected, suffers most from the decline and decay of bourgeois society...
>
> To find a solution to this impasse through art itself is impossible. It is a crisis which concerns all cultures, beginning at its economic base and ending on the highest spheres of ideology. Art can neither escape the crisis nor partition itself off. Art cannot save itself. It will rot away inevitably—as Grecian art rotted beneath the ruins of a culture founded on slavery—unless present-day society is able to rebuild itself.[54]

Without doubt, there is a powerful argument here, which cannot fail to strike a chord with any socialist sensitive to the symptoms of decay to be seen at every turn in the life of 20th century capitalism. Nevertheless, when the argument or rather the arguments are examined, flaws and problems immediately arise.

Lukács famously counterposed the totalising realism of Balzac and Tolstoy to the angst ridden fragmentation of Kafka, Joyce and Beckett. But even if one accepts Lukács's literary judgements (which I do not) this schema simply will not transfer to painting and sculpture. Far from 1848 appearing as the end of a great epoch of 'progressive' bourgeois realist painting it rather marks the start of a rich seam that produces Courbet, Manet, Monet, Sisley, Pissarro, Renoir, Lautrec, Cassatt, Morisot, Degas, Seurat, Van Gogh, Gauguin, Redon, Cézanne, Rousseau, Picasso and Matisse. Any notion of decline is even less applicable to sculpture. Rodin in the late 19th century was probably the most important European sculptor since Michelangelo, and the first half of the 20th century, with Brancusi, Moore, Kollwitz, Epstein, Picasso,

Calder, Hepworth, Gabo, Giacometti and others, must count as a sculptural golden age compared with the virtual desert of the 17th, 18th and early 19th centuries. Nor will Klingender's notion of the development from Impressionism to abstraction as a 'frantic flight from content, ie from social reality' stand up. Seurat's *Bathers* is a key step on the road to abstraction but it is not at all a move away from content or social reality (just the opposite in fact). In slightly different ways the same could be said of Van Gogh and Cézanne and, especially, of Cubism.[55] Trotsky's 1938 argument is different in that it doesn't share Lukács's or Klingender's condemnation of modernism, but the categorical nature of his pronouncements ('Art cannot save itself...it will rot away inevitably') is clearly a product of his general catastrophist outlook at this time. If the crisis of capitalism had developed as Trotsky expected[56] then art most certainly would have rotted away because all culture and civilisation would have collapsed, but it did not.

As well as these ad hoc objections there is a theoretical problem. The equation of decaying capitalism and bourgeoisie in decline with decadent declining art assumes a more mechanical relationship between base and this element of the superstructure than is warranted. In an earlier article in this journal I argued that art is an aspect of the superstructure least strictly determined by the economic base,[57] and Marx states:

> *It is well known that certain periods of highest development of art stand in no direct connection with the general development of society, nor with the material basis and the skeleton structure of its organisation.*[58]

Moreover when we examine the actual relation between the bourgeoisie and modern art we find that although the bourgeoisie certainly controls the art market and the art world it does not itself produce the art. The overwhelming majority of modern artists are not bourgeois but petty bourgeois.[59] What is more, they are petty bourgeois in revolt against the normal, alienated conditions of bourgeois and petty bourgeois life. As Trotsky says, 'Every new tendency in art has begun with rebellion'.[60] As rebellious petty bourgeois artists are inevitably influenced by oppositional ideologies and impulses from both right and left, with the influence of the left by and large outweighing that of the right. Nor is it the case that the bourgeois patrons of art in the 20th century have bought and promoted only art which embodied the ideological positions of the bourgeoisie. On the contrary, as Trotsky notes,[61] the bourgeoisie has taken pride in buying up and 'incorporating' art which challenges dominant bourgeois positions at certain points in time—for example, *Guernica* or even art which is sincerely anti-capitalist in its intentions and message, such as the work of Léger.

For all these reasons we must conclude that the historical decline of capitalism (provided it does not reach the acute phase of 'the mutual destruction of the contending classes' or the outright destruction of civilisation through world or nuclear war) does not necessarily lead to the decline of art. Perhaps Bertolt Brecht should have the last word on this particular point:

> MOTTO
> In the dark times
> Will there also be singing?
> Yes, there will also be singing
> About the dark times.[62]

There is, however, another and very different Marxist argument for contemporary art being in decline: that of Perry Anderson in 'Modernity and Revolution', his critical review of Marshall Barman's *All That is Solid Melts into Air*. Anderson pays fulsome tribute to the literary and artistic achievements of modernism in the early decades of the century and identifies the decline of art with the exhaustion of the European modernist impulse. Underlying this contention is a very precise *conjunctural* explanation of the advent of modernism:

> In my view, 'modernism' can best be understood as a cultural field **triangulated** by three decisive coordinates. The first...was the codification of a highly formalised academicism in the visual and other arts, which itself was institutionalised within official regimes of states and society still massively pervaded, often dominated, by aristocratic or landowning classes... The second coordinate is...the still incipient, hence essentially novel, emergence within these societies of the key technologies or inventions of the second industrial revolution: telephone, radio, automobile, aircraft and so on... The third coordinate... I would argue, was the imaginative proximity of social revolution.[63]

It was the combination of these three factors which provided modernism with its artistic charge but, Anderson argues, the Second World War brought this period to a definitive close. The old aristocracies were decisively displaced and bourgeois democracy established. Fascism arrived in force and 'the image or hope of revolution faded away in the West':

> The onset of the Cold War, and the Sovietisation of Eastern Europe cancelled any realistic prospect of a socialist overthrow of advanced capitalism, for a whole historical period. The ambiguity of aristocracy, the absurdity of aca-

demicism, the gaiety of the first cars or movies, the palpability of a socialist alternative, were all now gone... The post-war avant-gardes were to be essentially defined against this quite new backdrop. It is not necessary to judge them from a Lukácsian tribunal to note the obvious: little of the literature, painting, music or architecture of this period can stand comparison with that of the antecedent epoch.[64]

Anderson's analysis, as always, is erudite and elegant but (leaving aside the question of its historical accuracy regarding the genesis of modernism) as a perspective on the current and impending state of art it is open to major objections. One of the most important of these, the question of the 'Third World', Anderson is aware of but dismisses far too easily. He acknowledges that 'in the Third World generally, a kind of shadow configuration of what once prevailed in the First World does exist today', nods briefly in the direction of 'socialist revolution...already realised in 'Cuba or Nicaragua, Angola or Vietnam',[65] cursorily mentions the 'genuine masterpieces' of Marquez, Rushdie and Turkish film maker Yilmiz Güney, and then peremptorily dismisses the whole scenario in two sentences:

> Works such as these, however, are not timeless expressions of an ever-expanding process of modernisation, but emerge in quite delimited constellations, in societies still at definite historical crossroads. The Third World furnishes no fountain of eternal youth to modernism.[66]

This is all highly unsatisfactory. The term 'shadow configuration' is dubious to put it mildly; the 'socialist revolutions' are non-existent (and serve only to confuse matters here); *no* art works are 'timeless expressions' and *all* 'emerge in quite delimited constellations', and the art of the so called 'Third World' cannot be seen as either succeeding or failing in prolonging European modernism—we are talking about the large majority of the world's population and nations here. Above all one wants to say, 'What about...?' What about the films of Satyajit Ray or of Akira Kurosawa and other Japanese film makers? What about the new cinema of Africa and Latin America? What about the sculptors of Zimbabwe? What about the poetry of Pablo Neruda? What about Césaire and Senghor and the poets of négritude? The 'what abouts' continue to the limits of the reader's tolerance and the writer's knowledge.

The second major objection to Anderson's perspective points to an omission, a piece of historical amnesia, that is, on the face of it, astonishing. Anderson claims that 'hope of revolution faded away...for a whole historical period' and forgets...the 1960s (or more precisely the great upturn in struggle internationally that began in the 1960s and lasted till 1974). It is, of course, open to argument whether revolution was actually possible in May 1968 or in Chile in 1972-1973 or in Portugal in 1974 but not whether the 'image or hope' of revolution was 'in the air', or whether it had inspirational cultural effects. The 'what abouts' start again—Allen Ginsberg, Robert Lowell, Bob Dylan, John Coltrane, Joseph Beuys (and, as it happens, our old friend, Carl André of the bricks). For some reason Anderson remembers only Jean-Luc Godard.

Of course the explanation for this biographically amazing forgetfulness is Anderson's profound political miserabilism and pessimism which make him write off even the hope of workers' revolution both backwards and forwards, for the recallable past and the foreseeable future. This pessimism (and a certain high intellectual elitism) also makes him virtually deaf and blind to all those impulses and forces arising from below ('the signs in the street' as Berman calls them), which range from black power, women's liberation and flying pickets to punk, grunge and New Age travelling, and are crucial to both contemporary revolutionary politics and contemporary and future cultural creativity.

There is, therefore, no compelling reason to accept Anderson's 'closed horizon' and grim outlook for the arts. *Perhaps* he is right that *in Europe* 'little of the literature, painting, music or architecture of this period can stand comparison with that of the antecedent epoch' but even that limited judgement is not as 'obvious' as Anderson claims (there's Beckett, Camus, Pinter, Grass, Prevert, Solzhenitzin, Bacon, Kiefer, Tippett, Fried, Lessing, Fo, Greene and god knows who else to take into account) and it certainly doesn't apply to film (Bergman, Rossellini, Visconti, Fellini, Antonioni, Pasolini, Truffaut, Resnais, Godard, Wajda, Fassbinder, Tarkovsky, Losey, Loach etc) or, by definition, to television and video. Nor does it work at all for the United States where the postwar artistic achievement puts the pre-war arts in the shade in at least two areas: poetry (Ginsberg, Ferhinghetti and the Beats, Lowell, Frost, Plath, Rich) and above all the visual arts (Pollock, de Kooning, Rothko, Stella, Still, Newman, Rauschenberg, Johns, Warhol, Lichtenstein, Basquiat, Smith, Smithson, Serra, Kelly, Bourgeois, Judd, André, etc) and perhaps in three areas if we include modern jazz from Parker to Marsalis. If Anderson's theoretical foundation is flawed and his empirical judgement about the immediate past is, at the very least, open to question then we have no need at all to accept his foreclosure of prospects and possibilities in the immediate and not so immediate future even if capitalism is not overthrown in the next period.

To reject the argument, whether posed in Lukácsian, general Marxist or Andersonian terms, that art is in overall or inevitable decline is not to assert the opposite, that it is irresistibly in the ascendant. It is simply to suggest that at the present time there are too many variables, too many uncertainties to arrive at any definitive judgement. The perspective is open for both the arts as a whole and for the particular case of visual art. However, the corollary of this open perspective is that the record of human creativity being what it is we can reasonably expect to encounter late 20th and early 21st century masterpieces just as there are masterpieces from every century and half century since Giotto and the beginning of the Renaissance.

Conclusion

This article has been an attempt to tackle a series of questions that arise prior to the consideration of particular works of modern art, the most pressing of which was its legitimacy as 'art' at all. In the course of the discussion I have argued: (1) that the legitimacy crisis of modern art is not an accident or a conspiracy (despite the efforts of the media) or the fault of artists but is a historically and economically conditioned phenomenon; (2) that the arguments against modernist art's status as genuine art will not withstand critical examination and that by the best available Marxist definition of art the works of Picasso, Duchamp, André, Hirst et al are certainly art; (3) that it is a mistake to see modern art as especially obscure, inaccessible or unpopular; (4) that there are no good grounds for seeing modern art as in inexorable decline or incapable of producing great work today, tomorrow and the next day. Where then does this leave us standing, as it were, in front of the visual art of today?

It leaves us valuing art but hating the capitalist structure of the art world, its elitism, snobbery and commercialism. It leaves us defending art for its rebelliousness, its creativity and its human values while recognising that art as a privileged sphere of these qualities is the other side of the coin of a society which denies the vast majority creativity and humanity in their daily work and lives. It leaves us fighting to change that society and the art world it produces so that the art of the present and past can be appropriated by and accessible to all and so that in the future the art of the future will become the productive work of the future and the productive work will become the art. It leaves us facing the art of today not without preconceptions but without prejudice, responding to it with all the human faculties we can mobilise and understanding that at its best it retains the capacity to enrich and sustain us as human beings fighting for a better world.

Notes

1   This is only a restatement in relation to modern art of the classical Marxist position on the working class and traditional bourgeois art and culture as a whole. Thus Trotsky speaks of recommending Shakespeare and Pushkin to the workers. See L Trotsky, *On Literature and Art* (New York, 1977), pp67-69.

2   Cézanne and Gauguin were obviously direct influences and behind them we can trace Manet, Ingres, Goya and Velázquez. But this in no way diminishes Picasso's startling originality.
3   The shock of *Les Demoiselles* was not only caused by the formal innovations listed here but also by its 'content', its brutal depiction of the prostitute/client relationship (with all its implications for general sexual and social relations between men and women), and in this respect the painting remains genuinely shocking to this day.
4   See J Berger, *Success and Failure of Picasso* (Harmondsworth, 1965), p75.
5   Analytic Cubism, which lasted only three or four years (1910-1912), developed quickly to the point where traces of the depicted object(s) almost (but not quite) disappeared. Synthetic Cubism imported 'real' materials—oil cloth, newsprint etc—into the painting thus violating another tradition maintained since the Renaissance of the unity of materials in a work.
6   A 'ready made' upside down urinal signed 'R Mutt'.
7   There are isolated exceptions—Kurt Schwitters' 'sound poems', John Cage's *4'33"* of silence—but they have remained marginal to their respective art forms and do not change the general picture.
8   Though never, of course, its only function. Considerable caution must be exercised in the attribution of naturalistic representation to a tradition that ranges from Leonardo's *Virgin of the Rocks* to Hieronymus Bosch's *Garden of Earthly Delights* and Goya's nightmarish *Disparates*.
9   Anyone familiar with the Marxist tradition on cultural theory will detect the echo of Lukács here, but it will be evident I am not arguing a Lukácsian position here.
10 Society portraiture continues of course, as does a certain amount of art as state propaganda, but its quality and significance as art diminish dramatically. There is no artistically important painting of Napoleon III, Gladstone, Disraeli, Bismarck, Hitler or Stalin. (There was one portrait of Churchill—by Graham Sutherland—that could claim some serious artistic merit but this was destroyed by the Churchill family.)
11 *The Physical Impossibility of Death in the Mind of the Living*, to give it its full title.
12 Moreover this is a work which is too large for storage in any ordinary house and which involves considerable maintenance costs.
13 Which, in a delicious irony, it turns out is probably a fake.
14 Modern architecture, of course, has its own problem of legitimacy and public hostility.
15 See F Garcia Lorca, 'Theory and Function of the Duende' in *Obras Completas 3* (Barcelona 1997).
16 I must stress that this analysis has only addressed the question of why the crisis of legitimacy in modern visual art is especially acute. It has not addressed the wider problem of the general split between high culture and popular culture and working class philistinism which requires a much larger analysis of relations between class, exploitation, alienation and culture in capitalist society.
17 The most famous art faker of the century was van Meegeren who forged Vermeers.
18 Of course a Marxist and dialectician understands that all definitions are static concepts imposed on living, changing reality and that in the final analysis all definitions fray at the edges—there are always exceptions, transitional and marginal cases (like the coelacanth in biology). This does not change the fact that definitions are useful and necessary for human knowledge. 'Knowledge in general begins with distinguishing between things', L Trotsky, *On Literature and Art*, op cit, p64.

19 Think also of John Keats's lines: 'Beauty is truth, truth beauty/ That is all ye know on earth and all ye need to know.'
20 It is only these ready-mades which show an absence of craft skill. In Duchamp's other work, for example his Cubist/Futurist painting *Nude Descending a Staircase* (1911) and his 'sculpture' *The Large Glass* or *The Bride Stripped Bare by Her Bachelors, Even* (1915-1923), there is a very high level of technical skill.
21 It was the last of this integrated series. *Equivalent VIII* which, extracted from the total installation, became the infamous 'Bricks' in the Tate.
22 I should say here that, personally, I do find André's brick sculptures 'beautiful'. For an art historian who shares this view see P Wood, 'On Different Silences', *Museum of Modern Art Papers*, vol 2 (Oxford, 1996). However, I am not arguing that art has to be beautiful to be art, nor does the reader have to have my particular response to this work to accept my general arguments here.
23 Marcel Duchamp was an outstanding chess player who represented France in the Chess Olympics. In some ways his *Fountain* can be likened to a daring chess move in which he had calculated in advance the various possible responses of the art institutions, critics, journalists, public, etc.
24 A friend of mine visiting the 'Objects of Desire' exhibition at the Hayward Gallery touched Duchamp's *Bicycle Wheel* to see if it would spin and was immediately remonstrated with by the attendant. This despite the fact that the original *Bicycle Wheel* ready made (like the original *Bottle Rack* and *Fountain*) has been lost and what was being shown was a replica—a kind of authentic fake.
25 It is also reminiscent of Althusser's position that the proof of theory lay not in practice but within theory itself.
26 K Marx, *Wage Labour and Capital* (Moscow, 1978), p28. Also, 'Capital is not a thing, but rather a definite social production relation belonging to a definite historical formation of society', *Capital*, vol 3 (Moscow, 1966), p814.
27 K Marx, *Capital*, vol 1 (Moscow, 1970), pp76-77.
28 For a much fuller discussion of this idea from a position similar—though not identical to mine—see A Sanchez Vázquez, *Art and Society: Essays in Marxist Aesthetics* (London, 1979), especially 'Part II : The Fate of Art Under Capitalism'.
29 'Art is man's expression of his joy in labour,' writes William Morris in *Art, Labour and Socialism*, cited M Solomon (ed), *Marxism and Art* (Brighton, 1979), p85. Morris was broadly heading in the same direction as me, but without the advantage of having read Marx's *1844 Manuscripts*.
30 K Marx, *Early Writings* (London, 1963), pp124-125.
31 K Marx, 'Debating the Freedom of the Press', in L Baxandall and S Morowski (eds), *Marx and Engels On Literature and Art* (New York, 1974).
32 Cited in M Solomon (ed), op cit, p75.
33 L Trotsky, *On Literature and Art*, op cit, p96.
34 Ibid, p106.
35 Ibid, p114.
36 This argument raises the question of the so called 'interpretive' as opposed to 'creative' artist—the actor, musician, dancer, etc. These are transitional cases and normal usage of the term art in relation to such roles reflects this. Like all transitional cases they range from one end of the spectrum to the other—from the minimally artistic 'extra' or dancer in the chorus, to the highly artistic leading actor, prima ballerina, virtuoso violin soloist.
37 Once again there are transitional and intermediate cases: the work of theory like Marx's *Capital* or Trotsky's *History of the Russian Revolution* that has significant 'artistic' elements in its composition; the lovingly tended garden or carefully prepared meal that is a 'work of art'.
38 K Marx, *Theories of Surplus Value* (Moscow, 1963), Part I, p285.

39 By the same token the works in the Saatchi Gallery in St John's Wood are art but the advertisements produced by Saatchi & Saatchi are not.
40 Ortegay Gasset, T S Eliot and Ayn Rand represent versions of this right wing elitism. Adorno is the extreme example of left elitism. Clement Greenberg, the most influential art critic of the 1940s, 1950s and early 1960s, travelled from left elitism in *Avant Garde and Kitsch* in 1939 (called 'Eliotic Trotskyism' by T J Clarke) to right elitism in the 1950s and in his 1961 article 'Modernist Painting'; Luxemburg and Trotsky could also be seen as in the left elitist category because of their insistence on the impossibility of an independent working class culture under capitalism, but this is really an abuse of the term elitist.
41 T S Eliot, *The Use of Poetry and the Use of Criticism* (London, 1964), p150.
42 See T J Clark, 'Preliminaries to a Possible Treatment of Olympia in 1865', *Screen*, vol 21, no 1 (Spring 1980).
43 I leave aside here the fact that what it means to understand a work of art (especially visual art) is neither simple nor self evident.
44 It is worth noting that this useful information is not in any way the specialist knowledge of the art expert but was front page news at the time *Guernica* was painted. Moreover *Guernica* is very unusual in Picasso's vast oeuvre in needing this kind of factual explanation.
45 At the time the opinion was aired that the Republican cause would have been better served by a more 'accessible' Socialist Realist work but I can think of no Socialist Realist painting on any subject whatsoever that has had anything approaching the impact of *Guernica*.
46 The poem is called *On First Looking Into Chapman's Homer*.
47 See John Berger's critique of Picasso's paintings that are based on paintings by other artists in *Success and Failure of Picasso*, op cit, pp94-98, 183-186.
48 These and all other figures for attendance at the Tate were supplied by Joanna Stevenson of the Tate Gallery Information Office. Figures for the Hayward were supplied by Kate Harman from the Hayward Gallery and figures for the Royal Academy came from the press.
49 Attendance at the 'Sensation' exhibition ran at approximately 20,000 a week; at 'Objects of Desire' at approximately 8,000 a week. In the week ending 14 February 1998, Helen Fielding's *Bridget Jones's Diary* stood at number one in the paperback bestsellers list with a weekly sale of 22,371 and Ted Hughes's *Tales from Ovid*, the highest ranking poetry, stood at number 12 with a weekly sale of 6,680.
50 I have to confess I don't know any Italian painting of the 1890s or British sculpture of the 1790s. Undoubtedly there are people who know lots about both but they are as likely to be antique dealers as art critics or historians.
51 Thus we have the tale of Giotto drawing a perfect circle freehand, we have Raphaelesque Madonnas, we have Titian hair, we have Marx proclaiming that 'anyone in whom there is a potential Raphael should be able to develop without hindrance' [*Marx and Engels On Literature and Art*, (Moscow, 1976), p177] and we have Picasso saying, 'When I was a child I could draw like Raphael. I have spent the rest of my life trying to draw like a child.'
52 G Plekhanov, 'Art and Social Life' (1912), in P Davison, R Meyersohn and E Shils (eds), *Literary Taste, Culture and Mass Communication*, vol 3 (Cambridge, 1978), p63.
53 F Klingender, 'Content and Form in Art', in C Harrison and P Wood, *Art in Theory 1900-1990* (London, 1992), pp422-423.
54 L Trotsky, *On Literature and Art*, op cit, pp105-106.
55 See John Berger's analysis of Cubism in *Success and Failure of Picasso*, op cit, pp48-70.

56 See L Trotsky, 'The Death Agony of Capitalism and the Tasks of the Fourth International', in *The Transitional Programme for Socialist Revolution* (New York, 1977).
57 J Molyneux, 'Is Marxism Deterministic?', *International Socialism* 68, p55.
58 K Marx, *Introduction to a Contribution to the Critique of Political Economy*, cited in M Solomon (ed), op cit, p63.
59 I mean petty bourgeois in the strict Marxist sense of their objective role in the productive process of society and their relationship to the means of production. With very few exceptions artists are small producers who own their own means of production and sell not their labour power but the products of their labour.
60 L Trotsky, *On Literature and Art,* op cit, p104.
61 See ibid, pp104-105.
62 B Brecht, *Poems 1913-1956* (London, 1979), p320.
63 P Anderson, 'Modernity and Revolution', *New Left Review* 144.
64 Ibid.
65 Ibid.
66 Ibid.

Essays on Historical Materialism
Edited by John Rees

By the 1980s, bolstered by the growing popularity of postmodernism, the right wing critique of Marxism was well established. Notions of class were insupportable. The English and French revolutions were not revolutions at all and the Russian Revolution was a tragedy never to be repeated. In this book nine political activists and academics provide a devastating critique of the attack on the real Marxist tradition and provide a rigorous defence of the continuing relevance of Marx's method both in understanding the world and seeking to change it for the better.

£8.50, available from Bookmarks, the socialist bookshop
1 Bloomsbury Street, London WC1B 3QE
Phone 0171 637 1848, fax 0171 637 3616
email bookmarks_bookshop@compuserve.com

BOOKMARKS PUBLICATIONS

A respectable trade? Slavery and the rise of capitalism

A review of Hugh Thomas, **The Slave Trade: the History of the Atlantic Slave Trade 1440-1870** *(Picador, 1997) £25*

GARY McFARLANE

The transatlantic slave trade in Africans, reaching its height in the 200 years between 1650 and 1850, was of world historic importance. The rise of capitalist classes—eventually to be ruling classes—in the so called Western countries was in no small part due to the outlet the slave trade opened up for the investment of the cash surpluses accrued by merchants, as well as monarchs, aristocrats, guilds and clergy. The slave trade and its consequences still lie at the heart of the class antagonism behind the American dream: a country which, in its formative years was practically built by slave labour, also hailed itself as the first free republican government in the world and a haven for freedom loving Christians.

In Britain its legacy is there for all to see in the churches and wealth in the square mile of the City of London. Many of Britain's greatest institutions made their start on the back of the trade in Africans. The Atlantic ports of England, Bristol and Liverpool, acquired their economic importance and municipal grandeur as the direct instruments of the trade. London was the dominant port before the mid-17th century and remained the financial centre of the trade. But many smaller ports also had a hand in the trade, such as Lyme Regis, Portsmouth, Poole, Dartmouth, Falmouth, Exeter, Deal and Lancaster.[1] The investors in the South Sea Company, which in 1720 won the much prized *asiento*—the royal monopoly to trade 48,000 slaves annually for 30 years in the Spanish Empire—included many leading figures of the English ruling class of the day. 'Most of the House of Commons (462 members) and

100 members of the House of Lords (out of its total of 200) were included. So were Alexander Pope, Sir John Vanburgh, John Gay and all the royal family, including the bastards. The speaker of the House of Commons, Black Rod in the House of Lords and the Lord Chancellor were all on the list.'[2] Issac Newton lost £20,000 when the South Sea bubble burst, although the company went on to make fabulous fortunes for those not ruined by the speculative frenzy.

For such a monumental subject *The History of the Atlantic Slave Trade 1440-1870* is a very superficial book. Certainly Thomas is aiming to provide posterity with a definitive work on the subject. But from the introduction alone it soon becomes apparent that it is not so much a work of history as a political statement in defence of the British role in the trade. Indeed, we are asked to believe that the overthrow of the slave trade to the Americas was the result of the most moral foreign policies in British history[3], a policy implemented by the Royal Navy in the wake of the British abolition of the trade in 1808 and of slavery itself in 1833. Undoubtedly, Thomas has brought together a mass of material for the first time but it is in the cause of a bankrupt idea. The author fails to provide any real explanation for why the trade persisted in the age of freedom and reason except to claim that in the minds of Europeans it was merely a continuation of the traditions of Ancient Greece and Rome. In chapter two during a brief discussion of slavery in antiquity he repeats myths about Hamitic peoples in Africa and implicitly denies that the basis of Egyptian civilisation came from the interior of Africa:

> *Slavery was a major institution in antiquity. Prehistoric graves in lower Egypt suggest that a Libyan people of about 8000BC enslaved a Bushman or Negrito tribe. The Egyptians later made frequent attacks on their neighbours to the south.*[4]

He accepts that the Greeks and Romans were unprejudiced on grounds of race[5], but only provides examples of black people as slaves in the ancient world with the exception of a black herald who accompanied Odysseus to talk to Achilles, and a certain Aethiops, 'perhaps a black African freeman...present at the founding of Corinth.' Yet these are all mythical characters!

However, the crux of his argument is that it was the moral progressiveness of the north Europeans, in particular the British political establishment, which brought the trade to an end. Specifically, he states that it was a combination of a free press, the Quakers and the work of individuals from Montesquieu to Wilberforce. For Thomas the end of the slave trade came not because, as the French historian Claude Meillassoux put it, slavery as a means of production hindered agrarian and industrial growth, but because of the work of decent individuals.[6]

Thomas's interest in the subject began 30 years ago at a dinner where he met the Marxist historian Eric Williams and consequently was invited to read Williams's *Capitalism and Slavery*. Later in his own book Thomas tells us what he thinks of Williams's conclusions:

> *The memory of Dr Eric Williams may haunt the modern study of the Atlantic slave trade, but his shocking argument that the capital which the trade made possible financed the industrial revolution now appears no more than a brilliant jeu d'esprit. After all, the slave trading entrepreneurs of Lisbon and Rio, or Seville and Cádiz, did not finance innovations in manufacture.*[7]

Strangely, Thomas then provides in the next sentence a list of some of those who grew rich from slavery and did invest in industrial production.

There are some problems with Eric Williams' analysis but it still successfully nails the birth of capitalism to the banner of African slavery. Williams argues that Britain's 'triangular trade' provided a critical underpinning for the industrial revolution. He focuses on the British West Indies and not the entire system of slavery in the Americas. This has allowed Thomas, and others before him, to narrowly assess the level of profits made from slaving operations and conclude that this area alone could not have had such a critical impact on economic development. After all, foreign trade as a percentage of national wealth has been estimated at 10 percent for the mid-18th century. Profit rates derived from the plantations were massive, running at around a million pounds a year for the same period—a huge sum for the time but surely not enough to be the seed corn for what was to be the workshop of the world one hundred years later? But if we look a bit more carefully at the figures provided in Robin Blackbourn's *The Making of New World Slavery* we discover that the profits in question tripled between 1770 and the end of the century, precisely the span of years in which it is generally agreed that the industrial revolution began. In 1770 profits from the plantations contributed between 20 and 50 percent of the funds of fixed capital formation in the metropolis, depending on the estimates. Slavery was the major contributor to the primitive accumulation of capital no matter how shocking Thomas finds the idea. As Marx remarked in *Capital*:

> *The discovery of gold and silver in America, the extirpation, enslavement and entombment of the aboriginal population in mines, the beginning of the conquest and the looting of the East Indies, the turning of Africa into a warren for the commercial hunting of 'black skins', signalled the rosy dawn of the era of capitalist production. These idyllic proceedings are the chief momenta of primitive accumulation. On their heals treads the commercial war of the*

European nations, with the globe for a theatre. It begins with the revolt of the Netherlands from Spain, assumes giant dimensions in England's Anti-Jacobin War, and is still going on in the opium wars against China, etc.[8]

Adam Smith, who did not mention slavery in his *Wealth of Nations*, was against the institution for sound reasons of political economy which would have found him broadly concuring with Williams and the Marxists, as Thomas unwittingly shows:

Smith argued that the institution was just one more artificial restraint on individual self-interest. If a man had no hope of property, Smith thought, he would obviously work badly, for 'it appears...from experience of all ages and nations...that the work done by freemen comes cheaper in the end than that performed by slaves.' That sentence was immensely influential, but it was even less sustainable than Smith's contention that Irish girls had good complexions because they ate potatoes.[9]

But Marxists have to be careful not to assume the automatic superiority of wage labour from the point of view of the productivity of labour. In fact, for the sugar islands the balance may have been in favour of slavery up until the mid-19th century. It is important to see how capitalist relations battened on to and transformed a pre-capitalist mode of production. However, from the outset the sugar plantations in particular expressed organisationally the demands of generalised commodity production—the new, fledgeling and distant capitalist market. The six month harvest time in the Caribbean sugar fields brought forth the regimentation of the slave gangs to allow maximum pruduction and maximum envigilation. The process of refining the sugar itself required machinery and a power source—namely a mill, be it water, wind or horse driven, all co-ordinated in great detail. The whole business of running a plantation depended on credit. Planters were open to any innovation that might enable them to raise productivity, such as Eli Whitney's cotton gin, but they were selective. Ploughs, for example, never replaced hoes in the fields partly because of the relative cheapness of slaves measured against the surplus extracted but also because of the difficulties that slave control posed. The bills of exchange issued by planters and held by merchant creditors would be sold on, making them a principal financial instrument. In their turn manufacturers were to become the largest suppliers of credit to merchants in slaving ports like Liverpool and Bristol. In short, the plantation economy was concentrated at the heart of the new industries and commercial relations and was a primary motivator for the huge infrastructure developments such as harbours, docks and canals. The plantations' inputs (iron manufacturers, shipping) and outputs (cotton, sugar, tabacco) fertilised, in Williams's words, 'the most advanced areas of the economy' and the wealth it generated became the major source of working capital for an extended period.

At every turn Thomas reveals how the slave trade was vital to an immature British capitalism. In the decade of the 1730s Thomas estimates British ships carried 170,000 slaves to the Americas, overtaking the Portuguese. He shows how London then Bristol and, by the end of the 18th century, Liverpool are boosted, if not transformed, by the success of slaving. Thomas admits, 'The rise of Liverpool is a remarkable history, in which the slave trade played an important, perhaps even a decisive part'.[10]

The Bridgewater canal built between Liverpool and Manchester and opened in 1772 was made possible with slave money. Liverpool had already become an outlet for Manchester's manufactures such as cotton checks, a principal item of trade with west Africa. It had the effect, as intended by the merchants of both cities, of lowering transportation costs from 40 shillings by road to six shillings by canal for a ton of goods:

> The consequence was remarkable: Manchester's export trade was negligible in 1739, standing at £14,000 a year. Twenty years later it had increased to over £100,000, and by 1779 it stood at over £300,000. A third of this business went to Africa, principally items exchanged for slaves.[11]

Forgetting his implicitly anti-Marxist position, Thomas is forced to consider the possibilty of capitalist development through slavery.

> So it was that in 1780 the African trade in slaves seemed an essential part of the economies of all advanced countries, both a traditional thing and one which was being adjusted to meet all modern opportunities: the cotton cloth of Lancashire—above all Touchett's cotton checks, the very symbols of the new industrial process—were exported to secure African slaves.[12]

Throughout the 800 pages of this book you will not find any discussion of racism, surely a glaring omission given that the era bequeathed us the uniquely modern notion of discriminating against people on the basis of inherited characteristics. Thomas gives us the following justification:

> The slave trade was an iniquity. All the same, every historian must recall Hugh Trevor-Roper's warning: 'Every age has its own social context, its own climate, and takes it for granted... To neglect it—to use terms like "rational", "superstitious", "progressive", "reactionary", as if only that was rational which obeyed our rules of reason, only that progressive which pointed to us— is worse than wrong: it is vulgar'.[13]

Thomas seeks to offer no explanation as to how the ruling class, and others with a direct hand in the business, actually justified their actions. He looks almost in vain for critics of the trade among the educated classes of the day and concludes from the dearth of opposition that it was merely because it was almost a natural outgrowth of an old institution given a filip by the need to solve the labour shortage in the Americas: '...the reason why these humane doubts had no effect is surely to be accounted for by the memory of antiquity which dominated education and culture for the next three centuries'.[14] It is incredible that Thomas does not find it necessary to consider the development of racism as an ideology of justification and control created by a hugely exploitative system. It was the ideological expression of the shift from an ancillary slavery predominant in the Spanish Empire and in the early days of the English colonies, where slave labour was employed in a variety of endeavours, to systemic slavery centred exclusively on intensive plantation production of commodities.

Moreover, Thomas's assessment of the legacy of the trade for Africans and their descendants in the Americas and beyond is even more reactionary:

> *Like slaves in antiquity, African slaves suffered, but the character of their distress may be more easily conveyed by novelists such as Mérimée than by a historian. No doubts, though, the dignity, patience, and gaiety of the African in the New World is the best of all memorials.*[15]

In Thomas's account history becomes a chronology of events; pure empiricism stripped of analysis, and the voices of the direct producers. This is achieved by hiding behind an apparently value-free method, not seeking to impose 20th century ideas and models on the past, but just telling the story as it is. So the Atlantic slave trade is far removed from any discussion of racism because, supposedly, it was not an issue in the slaving countries of the day. Thomas concedes that Enlightenment thinkers such as Montesquieu and Rousseau were deeply hostile to slavery but nevertheless invokes the Enlightenment as part of the moral impulse that underlay the later undoing of the trade.

Despite his neutrality Thomas makes his prejudices clear enough in this assessment of the French Revolution and the real unity of interest that could be forged, albeit briefly, at the height of the revolutionary struggle, as the bourgeiosie, forced into desperate measures, aroused the majority at the bottom of society, including black people, against the aristocracy and the church: 'At the beginning of the revolution there were enough 'nègres' in Nantes for a black battalion, *Les hussards de Sainte Domingue*: they were a band of executioners, assassins, and pillagers who helped to make the city at that time one of the most bloody in France. Similar small populations of blacks survived in Bordeaux and La Rochelle'.[16]

The notion of slave rebellion undermining slavery is foreign to Thomas's outlook. In fact the San Domingo Revolution of 1792 in present day Haiti, which encompassed all the fears of metropolis and planters alike, struck the most powerful blow at slavery in conjunction with the unfolding revolution in France, but for Thomas it is just an aside to the parliamentary debates.

What ordinary people thought or did about the slave trade is not seriously considered by Thomas although, as he points out at the end of the book, the free press played an indispensable role in the abolition movement. However, the most consistently abolitionist element of this press came out of the tradition of pamphleteering and radical papers such as the *Political Register*, the *Black Dwarf* and later the Chartist *Northern Star*, which was the legacy of a revolutionary history from the mid-17th century. That tradition manifested itself in the most unlikely circumstances, such as in the slave crew riots in Liverpool:

> The crew of the *Derby*, given only 20 shillings when offered 30, rioted and were sent to jail. But that evening 3,000 sailors assembled, broke open the jail, released their friends, and stopped all ships, **even the slave ships**, from sailing. In the meantime, constables fired—seven were killed and 40 wounded. The sailors this morning again assembled, upwards of 1,000, all with red ribbons in their hats, and...about one o'clock assailed.[17]

Four were killed and the house of a big slave merchant, Thomas Ratcliffe, was ransacked.

Abolitionism in Thomas's account is ripped from its real place in history. This is paradoxical, given his attempt to ordain abolition's parliamentary leaders, and ultimately the British ruling class, with the laurels for victory over slavery. He fails to see how British mercantile and political interests were advanced by banning the trade: it was a statement of world hegemony, albeit not fully consolidated until the defeat of Napoleon. Nor does Thomas see the way political power was contested in Britain, which meant abolitionism became a rallying point for those at odds with the ruling order. The fact that the propagators of freedom at home were the enslavers of Africans abroad was not lost on the exploited labourers of England or France.

Robin Blackburn has offered a far more convincing analysis of the real motives of the British ruling class. They were involved in what they saw as a life and death struggle with revolutionary France. Napoleon's reintroduction of slavery in 1802 should have reasssured the British as it was just one example of how he was shearing the popular revolution of its radical implications. But for the British it provided the opportunity to pose as being against the slave trade and, by association, the French. After the war with France began, middle class reformers, of which the abolitionists were a section, had become afraid of raising issues of parliamentary reform lest they be condemned as traitors. The parliamentary abolitionists virtually dropped their campaign.

Napoleon's revival of slavery gave parliamentary abolitionists the chance to raise their heads without being seen as traitors. Britain could now pretend to be the enemy of the slave trade and block French attempts to re-establish their Caribbean sugar plantations, primarily San Domingo. As Robin Blackburn puts it, 'The vision of a pacified global system of commerce, so often proclaimed by abolitionists, had become the realisable objective of a single power'.[18]

Blackburn shows that in order to weld the population to their interests the Hanoverian oligarchy (ie the block of merchant capital and landed wealth that came together to install a monarchy agreeable to parliament in the 'Glorious Revolution' of 1688) was forced to look for popular legitimacy—this was the era of the birth of patriotism. Former enemies of abolitionism and reform now ran to its banner. In addition the period of the Napoleonic Wars saw a rising level of class struggle. The hundreds of thousands of signatures collected by the reborn abolition movement following Napoleon's reintroduction of slavery are testament to anti-slavery's ability to act as a lightning conductor for the latent and open antagonism between capitalists and landowners on the one side and independent producers and wage labourers on the other.

Wilberforce's victory, or more precisely the co-option of abolitionism, far from securing support for the ruling class at home, in fact led to a rising level of struggle from the growing class of wage labourers. Up until the first defeat of Napoleon in 1814 the government had to garrison 12,000 troops in the north of England. The fight against wage and chattel slavery went hand in hand. Centres of working class agitation were also abolitionist strongholds. Parliamentary, or middle class, abolitionism had a double-edged impact on these struggles:

> *Just as the abolitionist legislation helped the oligarchy to assert its right to rule and deflect middle class agitation for reform, so in the industrial districts middle class abolitionism helped manufacturers to outface menacing combinations, cement ties with other respectable persons and assert their social conscience. The Luddites sought to halt or deflect capitalist industrialisation by threats of violence; the abolitionists proclaimed the need to pacify relations and base them on a minimum respect for personal inviolability and autonomy. Abolitionism did not solve the problems of either government or employers,*

but it lent a more hopeful aspect to national sacrifice and discipline.[19]

Thomas furnishes us with much evidence to support the Marxist position as developed by Williams and Blackburn but draws none of the conclusions.

Notes

1   H Thomas, *The Slave Trade: The History of the Atlantic Slave Trade 1440-1870* (Picador, 1997) p206.
2   Ibid, p241.
3   Ibid, p590.
4   Ibid, p26.
5   Ibid, p27.
6   Ibid, p798.
7   Ibid, p795.
8   K Marx, *Capital*, vol I (Lawrence & Wishart 1977) p703.
9   H Thomas, op cit, p476.
10 Ibid, p246.
11 Ibid, p249.
12 Ibid, p285.
13 Ibid, p11.
14 Ibid, p795.
15 Ibid, p799.
16 Ibid, p254.
17 Ibid, p283.
18 R Blackburn, *The Making of New World Slavery* (Verso, 1997) pp309-310.
19 Ibid, p315.

REDWORDS PUBLICATIONS

Mutineers

Jonathan Neale

In the late 18th century the waterfronts of British ports were populated by the drunken, the desperate and the dispossessed. Many were press ganged or forced to choose between a harsh prison sentence and the navy—for others the navy was an attempt to escape from poverty. But the navy proved just as harsh a punishment as prison and poverty. Somehow, amidst the appaling brutality, ordinary men and women struggled to retain their humanity and, after revolution broke out in France, they found that courage and resistance were contagious and that heroism existed in unexpected places.

This is socialist fiction at its best

£8.99, available from Bookmarks, the socialist bookshop
1 Bloomsbury Street, London WC1B 3QE
Phone 0171 637 1848, fax 0171 637 3616
email bookmarks_bookshop@compuserve.com

The French Revolution: Marxism versus revisionism

A review of G Kates (ed), **The French Revolution: Recent Debates and New Controversies** *(Routledge, 1997) £14.99*

PAUL McGARR

'One's stance on the French Revolution inevitably reveals much about one's deepest ideological and political convictions'.[1] Gary Kates' comment, in his introduction to this collection of essays on the 1789 French Revolution, is certainly correct—though his claim is true of other great revolutions too. Even as the French Revolution was being fought out 200 years ago it was the subject of fierce arguments, which were centrally about the protagonists' own views on contemporary politics.

The English reactionary Edmund Burke first took up the cudgels in 1790 with his *Reflections on the Revolution in France*. In it he dammed the revolution and all its works. He attacked the whole notion of social change and reserved his worst venom for the 'swinish multitude'. Thomas Paine's famous *The Rights of Man* was written in reply to Burke and was enormously influential in the English radical and embryonic working class movements. But reaction then had the upper hand in England, and Paine had to flee to France to avoid arrest. Though the arguments today are conducted in a more subdued and academic manner, they remain as much about the politics of the participants as about the facts of the revolution.

For much of this century the idea that the French Revolution was a bourgeois revolution, driven by class conflict, which swept away the political structures of feudalism and cleared the way for the development of capitalism, was generally accepted. Not all those who advocated this view considered themselves Marxists but their interpretations of the revolution drew heavily on Marxism. The Marxist approach began with the

Second International leader Jean Jaures and was developed by people like Georges Lefebvre and Albert Soboul into the accepted orthodoxy. In recent years this 'orthodox' tradition has come under sustained attack from self styled 'revisionist' historians. This collection of essays edited by Gary Kates is a useful, if limited, guide to these debates. The first essay is a classic restatement of the 'orthodox' social interpretation by Albert Soboul. Readers of this journal will find little to disagree with here, though there are weaknesses which I will return to later.

The bulk of the book is concerned to spell out the revisionist case and some of what Kates calls 'neo-liberal' responses to the revisionists. The revisionists are represented in three essays by Colin Lucas, Keith Michael Baker and François Furet. Furet, a former member of the French Communist Party, was the doyen of the revisionists until his death last year. The core of the revisionist case can be summarised easily enough. It is that the revolution cannot be seen as a bourgeois revolution which destroyed feudal political structures. The revisionists insist that class struggle played little role in the revolution and that the revolution had nothing much to do with the development of capitalism.

The revisionists also argue that the nobility and bourgeoisie were part of a single ruling 'elite' of 'notables'—though they are woolly about what exactly is meant by these terms. This 'elite' was primarily made up of landowners and there was no fundamental social divide or conflict within it. Indeed all of the 'elite' were in favour of reform, and if only people had been a little more sensible, political reform was possible without social upheaval. The revolution thus becomes merely a squabble among this relatively homogeneous elite over political power, a squabble not rooted in any social base but fuelled by the 'autonomous political and ideological dynamic' of struggle between 'sub-elites', as Furet puts it.

This focus goes along with a turn away from seeing the revolution as having anything much to do with the underlying social conditions of the mass of people. 'What matters is not poverty or oppression,' Furet insists.[2] Instead we have to focus on the language, ideas and symbols of the revolutionaries and their opponents. This of course fits in with the wider trend in historical and philosophical writing variously labelled as 'the linguistic turn' or 'postmodernism'.

Keith Michael Baker spells out where this all leads. He denies 'that there are any social realities independent of symbolic meaning.' And he continues in the typically obscure language beloved of this school of historians:

> This is to argue that claims to delimit the field of discourse in relation to nondiscursive social realities that lie beyond it invariably point to a domain of action that is itself discursively constituted. They distinguish, in effect, between different discursive practices—different language games—rather

*than between discursive and nondiscursive phenomena.*³

This comes down to saying that talk of social reality is an illusion. The French Revolution, and indeed all historical events, are merely a clash between different languages, discourses and symbols. At least Marie Antoinette, the French queen at the time of the revolution, is reputed to have said to people hungry for bread, 'Let them eat cake.' Historians like Baker would more likely have claimed their hunger was mere talk. Richard Evans has written elsewhere about this approach to history, 'Auschwitz was not a discourse'.⁴ Neither was the storming of the Bastille—and Louis XVI certainly found out that Dr Guillotine's invention was more than talk or text.

It is amusing, reading the revisionist essays presented here, how often their own case is demolished by the evidence they present from their beloved discourses and texts. In addition, in the section entitled 'Neoliberal Responses to the Revisionists' there are several useful essays which demolish large chunks of the revisionist argument. Unfortunately, however, they do so without integrating their arguments into a wider understanding of the process of revolution. Indeed they often accept large chunks of the revisionist argument. So William Sewell, while demolishing the kind of nonsense from Keith Baker quoted above, insists at the same time:

> *I too have been influenced by the turn from social to intellectual interpretations of the French Revolution. I fully accept the revisionist critique of Lefebvre and Soboul and am convinced that the revolution cannot be understood apart from the language and conceptual vocabulary of the revolutionaries.*⁵

For this reason I will illustrate some of the good points made in the essays by Sewell, along with those by Colin Jones, Timothy Tackett and John Markoff, by restating what I believe is the correct general understanding of the revolution. The need to do this is further underlined by a weakness in the orthodox tradition, as exemplified here by Soboul. All the historians in this tradition drew on what they believed was some version of Marxism. Unfortunately it was really Stalinism. This meant a tendency towards a mechanical, deterministic approach. At times reading some of their work gives the impression that all was preordained, that history inevitably progresses and that, at the appointed hour, a revolutionary bourgeoisie with a fully formed consciousness of what it is fighting for springs up and seizes power. Too little room is left for conscious human intervention in making history. Not enough attention is paid to the fact that the consciousness of those engaged in the revolution developed in response to a crisis over which they had little direct control—and then went on developing in response to conflict and battles.

Fortunately Lefebvre, Soboul and others were good enough historians not to be totally derailed by these influences. Their work, especially on the movements from below, pulled in the opposite direction. Yet there is a tension between the real history and the distorted framework within which they tried to locate it. Another weakness was a tendency to overplay the 'unity of the Third Estate' against the old order in the revolution. Again the real history uncovered all the conflicts and divisions wonderfully. The limitations on different movements and how they affected the revolution were brought out. Yet this sat in a framework which stressed republican unity to an unwarranted degree. Of course it takes no leap of imagination to see how such an idea of an all-class alliance of the Third Estate against the old order fitted Stalinist popular front politics.

The main revisionist argument is that the revolution had no connection with the development of capitalism. Of course the development of capitalism and bourgeois revolutions are not the same thing. Capitalism had been developing long before the revolution. Reading the revisionists you could believe that nothing much was changing in France in the years before the revolution. They ignore the enormous social and economic changes that were going on in pre-revolutionary France. An indication of the scale of these changes can be given in a few figures. French trade grew by 400 percent in the 60 years before the revolution, iron production by 300 percent and coal by 700 percent. There is much more to it than that—but such figures are one reflection of a pace of change that seemed amazingly rapid to people at the time. One could add to the list the enormous transformations in agriculture in at least some areas of France, the development of transport links such as canals, the growth of ports and much more.

Such economic developments did not take place in a vacuum. They involved new relations between people, whole new ways of life, new classes—in short, the development of capitalism. And certainly capitalism also continued to develop after the revolution. The revolution itself, then, did not give birth to capitalism. Rather, it was a fight over political power and the nature and structure of the state. But the reason for that fight and the shape it took cannot be understood unless the way changes in society produced tensions within the existing state and political structures is grasped. And the state which emerged from the revolution was one which was refashioned in such a way as to further the development of capitalism—and the class which led the revolution, fashioned that new state and benefited from the new structures was the bourgeoisie.

T C W Blanning's book *The French Revolution, Aristocrats versus Bourgeois?* is hailed by one author in this volume as 'a major contribution to revisionism'.[6] Yet Blanning notes, 'It is both legitimate and necessary to look at what the revolution actually did. As soon as one does, one cannot help but be struck by the extent to which it furthered the interests of the bourgeois. At both a national and a local level it was they who benefited most from the new political arrangements'.[7] Exactly.

Revisionists argue that those who led the revolution and dominated the revolutionary assemblies were in fact often liberal professionals—lawyers and the like. Yet as Colin Jones points out, 'If one assumes that the liberal professionals who made up such an important constitutive part of the assemblies are socially autonomous from the economic bourgeoisie, then reforms as classically capitalist in character as the formation of a national market, the abolition of guilds, the introduction of uniform weights and measures, the removal of seigneurial excrescences, the redefinition of property rights come to be seen as the product of conspiracy, accident or hidden hand'.[8]

Revisionists like Furet, following earlier writers such as Alexis de Tocqueville, make much of the fact that the revolution 'completed' a process of centralisation and 'modernisation' of the French state that was already under way before the revolution. This is true, and the state that resulted was crucial in creating the conditions for the 19th century flowering of capitalism and industrialisation of France. But they assume that this process could, and in reality they mean *should*, have been carried through without any violent upheaval or revolution. There is no doubt the French monarchy did push for reforms but, as I will argue below, the path of reform was repeatedly blocked and the result was a revolutionary crisis. Only through the upheaval of the revolution was the refashioning of the state carried through. Of course history may have turned out differently, but we are seeking to explain what did in fact happen, not what later opponents of all radical social change would like to have happened.

The revisionists are right to say the bourgeoisie in France were often landowners, and that both nobles and the bourgeois were part of the 'ruling elite'. This is true in the sense that both bourgeois and nobles exploited the mass of the population. But to leap from that to the conclusion that there were no differences between the various elements of the exploiting classes is wrong. It reduces history to a simple tale of a crude division between one class, the exploiters, and another, the exploited. One will not get very far with such an approach in understanding any period of history.

In the years before the revolution in France there was a real growth in wealth based on commerce, manufacture and trade. And all landowners, noble or bourgeois, were increasingly producing for the market. Of course this all took place within the existing structures of society—how could it do otherwise? A landowner could be involved in commercial grain production, for instance, yet still be involved, directly or indirectly, in exploiting the range of feudal dues and privileges, internal tolls, taxes, monopolies and so on, to extract surplus rather than accumulating through investment in technical improvements. The same is true of the non-landowning bourgeois. In seeking to increase their wealth and position within society they would naturally attempt to exploit the existing structures in whatever way possible.

However, significant elements of the bourgeoisie were hindered by the privileges and restrictions imposed on them by those very structures. And many bourgeois, hit by noble monopolies, internal tolls, unequal tax burdens and so on, had a very material interest in the destruction of these structures. Above all, the idea that all the bourgeoisie were integrated within a single ruling elite alongside the nobility is simply false. Colin Jones quotes research which demonstrates the growing commercialisation and production for the market of French society in the decades before the revolt: 'The main intermediaries and beneficiaries of this growing commercialisation were the allegedly "traditional" [in the sense of being primarily landowners or office holders in the ancien regime] bourgeoisie.'

He also points out that despite the partial integration of elements of the bourgeoisie within the old political order and the nobility, the vast bulk of the bourgeoisie remained excluded. There were some 120,000 nobles in France in 1789. Yet, 'The size of the bourgeoisie grew over the century from 700,000 or 800,000 individuals in 1700 to perhaps 2.3 million in 1789. The new revisionist orthodoxy that bourgeoisie and nobility were somehow identical in economic terms thus seems rather wide of the mark'.[9] William Doyle, a leading revisionist, even suggests that these figures understate the real growth in the size of the bourgeoisie.[10] And the vast bulk of the bourgeoisie remained hampered by and excluded from the privileged orders of the existing social structures.

The revisionists, despite their intentions, cannot wish away the existence of real tensions among those they prefer to call the 'elite', including both the bourgeoisie and nobility. So Colin Lucas, for instance, admits 'the existence of very real antagonisms, divisions and antagonisms within this elite'.[11] This was certainly only too obvious to many who lived at the time of the revolution. To give one example, Emmanuel Sieyes wrote a famous pamphlet at the time of the revolution, 'What is the Third Estate?' He bitterly charged that:

> ...in one way or another all the branches of the executive have been taken over by the caste that monopolises the church, the judiciary, the army. A spirit of fellowship leads the nobles to favour one another in everything over the

rest of the nation. Their usurpation is complete, they truly reign.[12]

This may be a text or discourse, but as a simple matter of historical fact it struck a chord with the real experience of hundreds of thousands of people who knew it to be true. And for modern day academics who deny the role of the bourgeoisie in the French Revolution it is worth recalling that even Edmund Burke himself, who certainly knew a bourgeois when he saw one, viewed the French Revolution as the work of 'moneyed men, merchants, principal tradesmen and men of letters'.[13]

The revisionists do not deny that French society plunged into a huge crisis in 1789—facts can be stubborn things. So Lucas accepts 'the existence of a social crisis'.[14] And William Doyle argues that 'the French Revolution was neither inevitable nor predictable. What was inevitable was the breakdown of the old order'.[15] Even François Furet has to talk of how 'the revolution was born at the coming together of several series of events', above all 'an economic crisis (itself complex, being at once agricultural and industrial, meteorological and social) emerged alongside the political crisis which had existed openly since 1787'.[16]

This was also the near universal view of those who lived at the time—which while of course not something one should simply accept, certainly demands to be taken seriously. Calonne, a noble who became finance minister in the dying days of the old regime, summed it up in a way few historians, even revisionists, would disagree with: 'France is in its present condition impossible to govern'.[17]

There is not space here to go into the reasons for the crisis. The crucial aspect is the inability of the existing social and political structures to function any longer in a stable way. France, with its rickety and near bankrupt state structure and feudal survivals, faced growing external competition from already 'modernised' states where bourgeois revolutions had been carried through—above all, England and Holland. This amplified the growing tensions within France, between the growing bourgeoisie and the monopoly of state privilege and power held by the court, the nobility and, yes, by some—but not many—elements of the bourgeoisie.

There was also the growing tension between the mass of peasantry and those who lived off their backs, a burden which had been getting heavier in the years before the revolution, and the growing tension between rich and poor in the growing towns and cities. Furet may claim that 'what matters is not poverty or oppression'. This is not quite how it would have been seen by the urban poor in Paris in 1789—who in the months leading up to the revolution saw bread prices soar to their highest level of the 18th century, to the point where they had to spend some 88 percent of their income on bread alone. And I can imagine the reply to Furet's claim from the peasant who told an English traveller, 'May God send us something better for all these dues and taxes are crushing us'.[18] One is tempted to recommend a week without food to revisionist historians and then ask them if they still think poverty does not matter.

Virtually everyone at the time, and even revisionist historians today, accepted the need for *change* in France in the 1780s. The real argument was, and is, over what kind of change. It boils down, as ever, to reform or revolution. Was reform possible? Was it possible to create a 'modern' (ie capitalist) state, of the kind that did in fact eventually emerge in France, through some process of reform? In the abstract any answer is possible but the real history of France suggests that it was very unlikely—for the very simple reason that it was tried and failed. And this failure was rooted in the social structures of society, and cannot be reduced to an accident or the incompetence of this or that individual.

On several occasions the monarchy itself sought to push through radical reforms. The most famous was that in 1776 when the physiocrat minister Turgot wanted to open up trade, abolish guilds and reform the tax system to include taxing the privileged orders. The outcry from the privileged orders—the nobility and church—coupled with popular protest against the consequences of a free market in grain, saw the king back off and sack Turgot. The only way to push the reforms through would have been for the monarchy to attack the very aristocracy at whose head it stood, but that could open up a questioning of the whole social order, including the monarchy itself. The queen, Marie Antoinette, summed up the contradiction: 'The nobility will destroy us but it seems to me we cannot save ourselves without it'.[19]

It was another attempt at reform which finally sparked the revolution. As Furet's favourite historian Alexis de Tocqueville noted, 'Experience shows that the most dangerous moment for a bad government is generally that in which it sets about reform'.[20] The calling of the Estates General was an attempt to deal with the crisis by pushing through reform. In the context of that crisis it rapidly became the focus around which all the accumulated tensions in society erupted—tensions rooted in the real social conditions of real people.

Revisionists argue that the key in understanding the revolutionary events from 1789 onwards is politics and ideas. This is in one sense obviously true—how else do people organise, mobilise, even become conscious of their interests and aims? The revisionists, however, never ask why some ideas and some political groupings prospered while others did not. The reason is that ideas grow from, and are generalisations of, the real social experience of significant groups and classes in society. They are attempts to make sense of the social situation people find themselves in and point a way forward. Those ideas and groups that prosper are those that find an echo among real social forces, those which succeed in making sense of the world, and point a way forward, from the point of view of the real experience of particular groups and classes—and best help mobilise those forces.

Of course until a crisis in society opens the possibility of real change and throws people into struggle, both ideas and self-awareness of the interests of particular social groups can remain at best half formed. People will look for ways to adapt, not believing fundamental change is possible. Only in response to crisis and struggle do they become fully understood and expressed. So, for instance, Antoine Barnave, a leading figure in the early years of the revolution, had by 1792 developed one of the clearest analyses of the process. He wrote, 'ideas which had engaged me when they were still the object of fruitless curiosity absorbed me totally when public events began to suggest that there was some hope for them'.[21] Barnave then underwent a process of seeking to make sense of what was happening in the turmoil of the revolution, from the point of view of the bourgeoisie of which he was part. He ended up being guillotined, but while awaiting his fate in jail he wrote perhaps the clearest summation of the nature of the revolution penned at the time:

> *Once industry and commerce have begun to establish themselves the way will be open for a revolution in politics; a shift in the balance of wealth leads to a shift in the distribution of political power. Just as the possession of land once raised the aristocracy to power, so the growth of industrial property now raises the power of the people.*

Of course by 'people' he meant people like him, the bourgeoisie. Barnave went on, in a passage which is remarkable when one remembers this was written half a century before Marx developed his ideas:

> *One may from a certain point of view consider population, wealth, customs, knowledge as the elements and the substance which form the social body, and see in the laws and the government the tissue which contains and envelops them. If the tissue expands in the degree that the substance grows in volume the progress of the social body will occur without any violent commotion. But if instead of being an elastic force it opposes itself rigidly there will come a moment when proportionality will end and where the substance must be destroyed or where it must break its envelope and expand.*[22]

The revisionists point out that the nobility was agreed on the need for some real change in 1789. But they ignore the degree to which it simply was not prepared to surrender its power. So T C W Blanning gives a summary of the lists of grievances drawn up for the Estates General. He claims that it shows there was no real divide between nobility and the

Third Estate (which in practice meant the bourgeoisie) and that his table 'provides the revisionists with their best evidence'. One is tempted to say that with friends like this the revisionists hardly need enemies, as this 'best evidence' actually explodes the revisionist case. On issues such as equality before the law, abolition of arbitrary arrest, establishment of a constitution, equalisation of taxes and liberty of the press there is general agreement. But tucked away at the bottom of the table we find that on 'more economic freedom' there is a clear split between nobility and Third Estate. And, crucially, on 'abolition of seigneurial [ie feudal] rights' the Third Estate is against the nobility by five to one. Yet somehow Blanning, in common with other revisionists, argues that 'it is impossible to infer any confrontation'![23]

The Estates General met against the background of a social crisis with everyone agreeing the need for some kind of change. Social groups were, in this situation, forced to begin to articulate their interests in a new way. Figures emerged who put forward programmes for the reorganisation of society, pointed to a way out of the crisis. François Furet himself makes exactly this point, when he argues that in the revolution people were putting forward ideas which sought 'to reconstruct through the imagination the whole social edifice which had fallen to pieces'.[24]

Some of the bourgeoisie was too tied into the existing structure of society to look for any radical change. But a large part of the bourgeoisie had everything to gain from breaking the old structures and began to rally around various programmes for change. They did so in the face of determined opposition from the old order—a point consistently ignored by the revisionists. It was the nobility and king who refused, until forced to accept, the demand for all to meet together in one assembly instead of preserving the privileged orders' own assemblies. It was the king who tried to cow the Third Estate by decreeing, 'The king wishes the ancient distinction between the three orders of the state to be preserved in its entirety as being essentially linked to the constitution of his kingdom'.[25] To ram his point home he had the hall where the deputies were meeting ringed with armed royalist troops.

All this was taking place against the background of growing revolt from below. It was this volatile situation which spilled over into revolution on 14 July 1789. There is not space here to go into the development of the revolution itself, but the same pattern is there throughout. There is long and determined opposition from the old order—including armed counter-revolution and support for the foreign armies that sought to crush the revolution. There are those among the bourgeoisie who wanted some change but pushed for a compromise with the old order, and there are those who come to see the only solution as much more radical change. All the while there is the pressure from below, in town and country, as vast numbers of ordinary people try and take matters into their own hands.

The revisionists reduce the political conflicts to 'elites' fighting for power. Yet millions of people were engaged in real social conflict. Programmes for social and political change put forward by minorities grew out of such conflict and developed through it. They could only gain support if they reflected the real interest of significant social forces. The revisionists fail to ask why some programmes were taken up and others not—after all, there were countless schemes put forward.

Let me underline the key role played by opposition from the old order, which is always ignored by the revisionists. Timothy Tackett in his 'Nobles and Third Estate in the National Assembly' brings this out very clearly. He shows that from the very beginning of the revolution the nobility wanted to block real change. He quotes a series of letters from 'moderate' members of the Third Estate in the assembly who were pushed 'left' because the nobles 'refuse to yield an inch of ground'. Jean Baptiste Grellet de Beauregard wrote, 'Those who have led the nobles have blocked all roads to compromise.' Laurent de Visme wrote in his diary that he had opposed radical measures at first but had changed his mind because 'the nobles' actions have justified it'.[26]

Such debates took place in the context of the upsurges from below and mass mobilisation. Even Furet admits that the revolution 'was characterised in fact by an exceptional mobilisation of the habitually inert social forces'.[27] John Markoff's useful essay 'Violence, Emancipation and Democracy' documents the huge peasant upheaval. The impact of such popular revolt on shaping the policies and programmes of those in the assembly is well known. Markoff underlines the point simply and well by quoting the caustic remark of one radical deputy in the National Assembly on seeing former opponents of change shifting their position: 'Severed heads were frightfully instructive'.[28]

The refusal of the old order ever to give up its hopes of a counter-revolution eventually led to a situation in which the search for a stable compromise broke down. It was that which created the conditions in which a minority of the bourgeoisie, the Jacobins, were able to put forward a programme for uncompromising fight to the finish. 'Liberty or death' was their slogan, around which significant social forces rallied. That involved the Jacobins allying themselves with sections of the popular urban movement and making huge concessions to the peasant revolts too. Out of this they led a revolution which smashed the old order entirely.

The victory of the revolution elevated the bourgeoisie from an oppressed junior partner in the exploiting classes to the dominant class in society. And with this went a state and legal structure that reflected their interests. Those who reject the connection between the political conflicts in the revolution, class struggles, the outcome of these and the further development of capitalism, should set themselves a simple task: try and imagine the mid-19th century industrialisation of France taking place with the essential structures of the old regime still intact.

The revisionists' real argument is not so much about what happened in France 200 years ago but about their opposition to revolution in general. François Furet denounced the revolutionaries of two centuries ago because they tore 'France away from its entire past', 'revoked' everything that had been done in previous centuries and set out on 'the immense and utopian ambition to create an entirely new social order and a new set of institutions'.[29] Furet declared 'the revolution is over', meaning there was no longer any need for radical social change—repeating the exact slogan of the Feuillants, a right wing faction of the bourgeoisie in France in the 1790s. Furet commended the capitalist 'market society' because competition leads to balance. And he declared himself delighted that Frenchmen no longer believe that in order to change society you have to take over the state by force.[30]

It is clear such arguments have more to do with current politics than with history. In fact they are little more than a nicely dressed version of Burke's tirade against fundamental social change and revolution. Furet and the revisionists want to bury the notion of revolution in history—to abolish its spectre today. While some of the essays in this book demolish the details of the revisionist historical case, they unnecessarily accept far too much of the revisionist framework.

Let me conclude by quoting the view of Michael Kennedy, a historian who has made a massive study of the Jacobin clubs that were at the heart of the French Revolution. Despite his approval of François Furet's revisionism, Kennedy concludes, 'Nevertheless my own studies of the clubs have led me to the conclusion that there is much truth in the radical-Marxist view of the revolution, that class conflict was, indeed, a major determinant'.[31]

Notes

1. G Kates, in G Kates (ed), *The French Revolution: Recent Debates and New Controversies* (Routlege, 1997), p1.
2. F Furet, ibid, p84.
3. K Baker, ibid, p146.
4. R Evans, *In Defence of History* (Granta, 1997), p124.
5. W Sewell, in G Kates (ed), op cit, p144.
6. C Jones, ibid, p182.
7. T C W Blanning, *The French Revolution: Aristocrats versus Bourgeois?* (London, 1987), p42.
8. C Jones, in G Kates (ed), op cit, p178.
9. C Jones, ibid, p165.
10. W Doyle, *Origins of the French Revolution* (Oxford, 1980), pp129, 231.

11   C Lucas, in G Kates (ed), op cit, p51.
12   Quoted in P McGarr, 'The Great French Revolution', *International Socialism* 43 (1989), p23.
13   Quoted in C Jones, in G Kates (ed), op cit, p177.
14   C Lucas, ibid, p52.
15   W Doyle, op cit, p210.
16   F Furet, in G Kates (ed), op cit, p85.
17   Quoted in P McGarr, op cit, p128.
18   Ibid p29.
19   Ibid p27.
20   Ibid p28.
21   Ibid p92.
22   Quoted ibid, p101.
23   T C W Blanning, op cit, p23.
24   F Furet, in G Kates (ed), op cit, p85.
25   Quoted in P McGarr, op cit, p31.
26   T Tackett, in G Kates (ed), op cit, p198.
27   F Furet, ibid, p80.
28   Quoted in J Markoff, ibid, p201.
29   Quoted in P McGarr, op cit, p94.
30   Ibid p94.
31   Quoted ibid, p104.

A Socialist Review

Edited by Lindsey German and Rob Hoveman

This book contains 59 articles, debates and reviews previously published in **Socialist Review**, Britain's biggest selling socialist monthly magazine. Topics covered range from the rise of New Labour to the real history of the monarchy, the life of Malcolm X to the Gulf War, the end of apartheid to the rise of Le Pen and from women's liberation to postmodernism. The book demonstrates the strength and breadth of the real Marxist tradition. It will be accessible to those new to politics and history and provide a mine of information to any reader.

£9.95, available from Bookmarks, the socialist bookshop
1 Bloomsbury Street, London WC1B 3QE
Phone 0171 637 1848, fax 0171 637 3616
email bookmarks_bookshop@compuserve.com

BOOKMARKS PUBLICATIONS

Will the real James Connolly please stand up?

A review of James Connolly, **The Lost Writings***, introduced and edited by Aindrias Ó'Cathasaigh (Pluto Press, 1997) £13.99; and James Connolly,* **Selected Writings***, introduced and edited by Peter Berresford-Ellis (Pluto Press, 1997) £12.99*

SHAUN DOHERTY

The publication of selections of Connolly's writings could not be more timely. To make sense of the current attempts at political accommodation in the North of Ireland it is essential to re-examine the history of resistance to Britain's involvement in the country as a whole. Central to that re-examination are the life, writings and political legacy of James Connolly, Ireland's pre-eminent Marxist.

Connolly had predicted that the partition of Ireland proposed by the British prime minister, Asquith, in 1914 and agreed by the leaders of the Irish Nationalist Party, Redmond and Devlin, would be 'a betrayal of the national democracy of industrial Ulster, would mean a carnival of reaction both North and South, would set back the wheels of progress, would destroy the oncoming unity of the Irish labour movement and paralyse all advanced movements while it endured'.[1]

Partition of the six counties of Ulster and the creation of the Northern Irish state eventually occurred in 1921, five years after Connolly's execution following the 1916 rebellion. The legacy of partition has been the creation of a sectarian state within which the Nationalist minority has been systematically oppressed and discriminated against and the working class as a whole divided on material and religious grounds. Political conflict has endured with varying degrees of intensity for the whole of its existence. Since 1968 that conflict has taken the form of a mass civil rights campaign, the deployment of British troops and military repression, the subsequent emergence of the

Provisional IRA and a campaign of armed Republican resistance, sustained sectarian attacks by Loyalist murder gangs, and most recently a fragile ceasefire and an attempt to arrive at a political settlement through a 'peace process'. Throughout the whole of this period the political leaders of the Unionist majority have been intransigent in their opposition to progress or any attempt to circumscribe their positions of power and privilege. Indeed, it could be argued that this intransigence is testimony to their inability to offer Protestant workers any vision of a better future let alone any significant material benefits. In these circumstances it is in their interests to fan the flames of sectarian conflict. Connolly would have taken little comfort from the accuracy of his prescient analysis:

> *Let us remember that the Orange aristocracy now fighting for its supremacy in Ireland has at all times been based on a denial of the common human rights of the Irish people; that the Orange Order was not founded to safeguard religious freedom, but to deny religious freedom and that it raised this religious question, not for the sake of any religion, but in order to use religious zeal in the interests of oppressive property rights of the rack-renting landlords and sweating capitalists.*[2]

Northern Ireland's industrial strength of 1921, with its shipyards, heavy engineering and linen industries, has long since disappeared. But the political monsters unleashed by Britain to police it nearly 80 years ago live on. Although they represent a movement that is rapidly fragmenting and an ideology in acute crisis, Ulster Unionist politicians will continue to obstruct any kind of political progress and are still using the Orange card to keep workers divided. The way they have whipped up sectarianism at Drumcree and elsewhere with the spurious justification of protecting Protestant 'culture' and 'civil liberties' is testimony to their historical role. Connolly's description 84 years ago could not have been more relevant than it is today.

At the same time, however, the strategy being adopted by the Provisional IRA and its political wing, Sinn Fein, in the current phase of the struggle stands in sharp contrast to the positions adopted by Connolly on all of the central issues. Militant Republicanism has dominated the resistance to the British presence since 1971, but neither its strategy of armed struggle nor its pursuit of an elusive 'peace process' is able to deliver a solution. They themselves recognise that a military victory is not possible and that their unarmed strategy is dependant on alliances with ruling class political parties in Britain, the United States and Southern Ireland.

In a document circulated by the Republican leadership in 1994 they make this quite explicit:

> The strategic objectives come from the prolonged debate, but are based on a straightforward logic: that Republicans at this time and on their own do not have the strength to achieve the end goal. The struggle needs strengthening most obviously from other Nationalist constituencies led by the SDLP, Dublin government and the emerging Irish-American lobby.[3]

This approach has led to the adoption of the Mitchell principles which accept de facto the continuation of partition. Indeed, the pursuit of the US lobby led them to court Clinton himself at the time when he was contemplating a bloody carnage in the Gulf. Their policy has also led to an acceptance and consolidation of the divide between Nationalist and Loyalist communities which negates the possibility of an appeal to their common class interests.

It would be stretching imagination beyond any reasonable limits to claim that the Republicans of today have inherited the mantle of Connolly—Connolly who organised among Catholic and Protestant workers alike and led them together against the employers, Connolly the principled revolutionary who stood out against the imperial slaughter of the First World War alongside Lenin and the Bolsheviks, Connolly the implacable opponent of reformism who castigated the French socialist Millerand for entering into a coalition government in 1899 that included Galifert, the butcher of the Paris Commune.

One of the greatest benefits of engaging with Connolly's own writings is the light they shed on the struggle today and the extent to which they expose any resistance which does not put the working class at the centre of the stage. Pluto has re-issued the Berresford-Ellis collection first published by Pelican in 1973. The Pelican edition was the first introduction to Connolly's writings for many of us who had become involved in the most recent phase of the Irish struggle following the civil rights movement of 1968. The O'Cathasaigh selection is an attempt make available some of the extensive body of Connolly's work that has been hidden in the National Library of Ireland. No edition of Connolly's collected works has yet appeared. Both books should be warmly welcomed, but Berresford-Ellis in the Introduction to his volume exemplifies a crucial problem.

Connolly's writings are an important part of his political legacy. Although not primarily a theoretician, Connolly was an outstanding propagandist and polemicist and one of the most effective popul2risers of socialist ideas. Both these volumes provide valuable examples of his work, but the way these examples are selected and introduced is problematic. Just as different political traditions have fought over Connolly's corpse, every attempt to publish his writing has reflected the political stance of its editors. Some have sought to portray him as a Catholic socialist and others have sought to use those extracts from his work which supported their political agendas at the expense of Connolly's own. Berresford-Ellis is no exception. He takes an uncritical attitude to Connolly and implies that his involvement in 1916 was the fitting culmination of his political life.

In his Preface to the 1997 edition of *Selected Writings* Berresford-Ellis laments the lack of a comprehensive collection of Connolly's writings and presents a brief summary of the published assessments of his political contribution. He quite rightly identifies attempts to appropriate Connolly for 'revisionism' and singles out Austen Morgan's *James Connolly: A Political Biography*.[4] Morgan argues that Connolly lived as a socialist, but died an Irish Nationalist and that his death was a denial of his life's work. Morgan used this assessment to provide left cover for his rejection of Irish Republican resistance and his apologia for British involvement in Ireland. But Berresford-Ellis attempts to appropriate Connolly for the opposite tradition, the tradition which has sought to prioritise the Nationalist struggle over any other and has seen any analysis based on class as subservient to it. This form of the 'stages' theory is the mirror image of Morgan's. It is most famously articulated in C Desmond Greaves' *The Life and Times of James Connolly*.[5] It argues that the struggle for the socialist transformation of Ireland has to await its national liberation. In his Preface to the 1985 edition of *The History of the Irish Working Class* Berresford-Ellis writes, 'In Ireland today, as in previous centuries, the mainspring of socialism is in the national struggle'.[6]

This starting point leads to an inevitable distortion of Connolly's life and work, but ironically also results in an uncritical assessment of it. If the 'mainspring' is the national struggle then the tendency will be to prioritise Nationalist politics at the expense of the socialist objective. Or to put it in the words of Éamon de Valera, one of the Republican heroes of 1916 who subsequently became Fianna Fail prime minster, 'Labour must wait.'

In any evaluation of Connolly's work there needs to be a clear understanding of the tension between his lifelong commitment to working class struggle and his relationship to the fight for national liberation. This tension is not just theoretical. The historical developments during the last three years of his life shaped his attitude considerably. From 1889 he had been a socialist and trade union organiser in Scotland; in 1896 he moved to Ireland and formed the Irish Socialist Republican Party; in 1903 he left for the US where he became involved with the Socialist Labour Party and subsequently became an organiser for the

International Workers of the World; finally he returned to Ireland in 1910. In 1911 he became organiser for the Irish Transport and General Workers Union in Belfast and then its general secretary in 1913.

Dublin 1913 proved to be a watershed. The lockout of the Dublin working class as the employers fought to prevent the unionisation of workers and to stem the increasing influence of Connolly's union ended in defeat for the workers. The solidarity shown by rank and file workers in Britain was outweighed by the capitulation of their union leaderships and the TUC-backed campaign of scabbing.

This defeat was followed in 1914 by the outbreak of the First World War. Connolly was in a small minority of the international socialist organisations in opposing the war and the ITGWU campaigned against conscription. He believed that the war presented revolutionaries with an opportunity, particularly in Ireland, to strike a blow against the biggest imperial power in the world: 'Starting thus, Ireland may yet set a torch to a European conflagration that will not burn out until the last throne and last capitalist bond and debenture will be shrivelled on the funeral pyre of the last warlord'.[7] In order to follow through this belief he formed an alliance between his Irish Citizens Army and the Nationalist Irish Volunteers that led to his central role in the armed uprising of Easter 1916.

The relationship between these three momentous events exposed the weaknesses as well as strengths of Connolly's politics. The conclusions he drew from the defeat of 1913 and the outbreak of war the next year undoubtedly contributed to his involvement in the Easter rising. Out of the defeat of working class struggle and the carnage of war he became increasingly drawn to the idea of armed revolt against Britain in alliance with the forces of Nationalism. He hoped that such a revolt would not only challenge British rule in Ireland but would inspire workers' resistance to the war throughout Europe.

In order to understand this relationship it is necessary to adopt a critical evaluation of Connolly's approach to the national question. Here we part company with Berresford-Ellis. Connolly's alliance with the Nationalists in 1916 had its roots in his analysis of the historical role of bourgeois nationalists. In his most important and insightful book, *Labour in Irish History*, Connolly contrasts the role that workers' struggles have contributed to the fight against British imperialism with the dominant oppositional politics of Irish Nationalism.

In his introduction to the 1987 Bookmarks edition of *Labour in Irish History*[8] Keiran Allen argues that Connolly's view that capitalism in Ireland could not achieve prosperity by establishing a manufacturing system in a world market led him to a blind spot where Republican views on economic development were concerned. Because he believed that the struggle for Irish independence led to an assault on capitalism itself, he did not recognise the extent to which even militant Republicans could contribute to capitalism's survival. Instead he argued that if militant Republicans broke with the constitutional Nationalists they would be inevitably drawn towards socialism.

The best example of how there could be a pull in the opposite direction, how there could be two way traffic on the bridge between Republicanism and socialism, is provided by James Stephens, one of the co-founders of the Fenians in 1858. Even though he was a socialist and a member of Marx's First International, so wedded was he to the notion of an all-class alliance to free Ireland that he regarded any attempt to raise social issues within the Fenian movement as lunatic. Socialism was simply a matter of personal preference. The unity of the Nationalist movement was what mattered to the exclusion of all else.

The beauty of *Labour in Irish History* is the way in which Connolly exposes this notion. Nationalists like Sarsfield, Grattan and O'Connell all feared the masses more than the British. Any movement from below that threatened their own class position and material wealth was to be vehemently opposed. Consequently the Irish bourgeoisie had a record of cowardly betrayal which Connolly ultimately traced to their weak manufacturing base and their need to take more drastic measures than they were prepared to against the landed aristocracy and all those dependent on Britain for protection. He describes the Act of Union with Britain in 1800 being made possible '...because Irish manufacture was weak and consequently had not an energetic class with sufficient public spirit and influence to prevent the union'. The constitutional Nationalists argued the opposite. If only they had their independence then the economy would flourish.

The weakness of the book, however, lies in Connolly's distinction between the old Home Rule tradition of constitutional Nationalism and militant Republicanism. Fintan Lalor and John Mitchel are hailed as revolutionaries even though the former defended the rights of private property and the latter was horrified when the workers began to take the initiative in the French Revolution of 1848. His failure to understand the common ground within which the traditions of constitutional Nationalism and militant Republicanism were rooted had tragic consequences not only in the years following his death, but for the struggle today.

I have set out this argument at some length because Berresford-Ellis makes an intemperate attack on Allen's Introduction and a shameful comment on Trotsky's attitude to the 1916 rebellion. He expresses his delight at the Bookmarks publication of *Labour in Irish History*, but has his delight tempered by:

Kieran Allen's introduction, which tried to claim that Connolly was really a Trotskyist at heart. As Trotsky singularly failed to grasp the meaning and significance of the 1916 uprising in which Connolly fought and gave his life, one might accuse Allen of having a cruel sense of humour. Allen disagreed with Connolly's principal teachings and urged his readers to ignore them. One wondered why he had bothered to write the introduction to the work at all.[9]

To start with the last point first. It was precisely because Allen wanted to highlight the whole of Connolly's work and not just those sections of it which appeared to justify the Republican embrace that he not only wrote the Introduction referred to above, but also wrote *The Politics of James Connolly* (Pluto, 1990), a political biography that highlights Connolly's contribution to the revolutionary tradition in Ireland. In fact, the Introduction to *Labour in Irish History* pays tribute to Connolly's achievement in laying the foundation stone for a revolutionary socialist strategy in Ireland and argues that his insights place him head and shoulders above many later left wing theorists who have sought in vain to find allies among progressive sections of the Irish upper class. The idea that Allen tries to claim Connolly for the Trotskyist tradition is refuted by the conclusion to *The Politics of James Connolly*: 'Although Connolly cannot be claimed for any particular Marxist tradition, he belonged primarily in the revolutionary camp'.[10] The strength of Allen's contributions is that they pay Connolly the respect of critical analysis and depart sharply from the hagiographical tones of Greaves and Berresford-Ellis.

There is indeed a connection between Connolly's insights in *Labour in Irish History* and Trotsky's theory of permanent revolution. They both argued that only the working class could be relied upon to fight consistently against imperialism. Connolly puts it explicitly: '...only the working class remain as the incorruptible inheritors of the fight for freedom in Ireland.' Particularly in a backward country with a weak bourgeoisie the working class could be crucial. But an insight, however valuable, is not a fully developed theory, and key elements in Trotsky's theory are missing from Connolly, in particular his argument that the struggle could only be successful if it led to the establishment of a workers' state. Connolly mistakenly implies that if only constitutional Nationalism is rejected a more militant Republicanism might become the vehicle for social advance. A consequence of this belief was his failure to establish an enduring socialist organisation independent of Republicanism.

Secondly the allegation about Trotsky's attitude towards 1916 is quite wrong. Indeed, in his own Introduction to *Selected Writings* Berresford-Ellis quotes Trotsky's response to Plekhanov's 'wretched and shameful' remarks about the harmful effects of the uprising. It is true that Trotsky did not have as sophisticated a position as Lenin and he thought that 1916 represented the end of the national uprising and ushered the proletariat onto centre stage. But he was as unequivocal in his defence of the uprising as he had been critical of the British trade union bureaucracy's role in the 1913 Dublin Lockout. Lenin's more accurate formulation describes the situation in Ireland as follows: 'For to imagine that social revolution is conceivable without revolts by small nations in the colonies and in Europe, without the revolutionary outbursts of a section of the petty bourgeoisie with all its prejudices...to imagine that means repudiating social revolution... Whoever expects a "pure" revolution will never live to see it'.[11] Both Greaves and Berresford-Ellis mistakenly use this quote to justify the cross-class Nationalist alliance within which socialist aspirations would be subordinated to the struggle for national liberation. But Lenin was not articulating a carefully thought out strategy for the revolutionary struggle in Ireland; he was rightly making a principled internationalist statement of support for an anti-imperialist revolt which many other prominent socialists had repudiated.

Lenin himself was won over to Trotsky's theory of permanent revolution in the months leading up to the October insurrection in Russia and no one could accuse him of having illusions in what 1916 had achieved. Indeed he argued, 'The misfortune of the Irish is that they have risen prematurely when the European revolt of the proletariat has not yet matured. Capitalism is not so harmoniously built that the various springs of rebellion can of themselves merge at one effort without reverses and defeats'.[12]

Lenin had also conducted a polemic in his *April Thesis* against the 'old Bolsheviks' who retained a schematic belief in the need for a bourgeois democratic revolution to be completed before a proletarian revolution. He argued that the actual experience of the struggle in Russia after the February revolution demonstrated an 'interlacing' of one struggle with another and the creation of a situation of 'dual power'. Alongside the Provisional Government of the bourgeoisie another government had emerged, the Soviets of Workers' and Soldiers' Deputies.[13] Any notion that he was downplaying the importance of workers' involvement and socialist objectives in anti-imperialist struggles is nonsensical.

It is also important not to lose sight of the fact that Connolly's involvement in 1916 did not mean that he had abandoned his belief that the working class was the key to the successful emancipation of Ireland. He was realistic about the chances of success, but he knew that even if the uprising was to triumph there would be other struggles ahead. In a speech to the Irish Citizen's Army he spelt it out:

> The odds are 1,000 to one against us. If we win we will be great heroes; but if we lose we will be the greatest scoundrels the country has ever produced. In the event of victory hold on to your rifles, as those with whom we are fighting may

stop before our goal is reached. We are out for economic as well as political liberty.

Greaves and others describe his alliance with the Volunteers as a sign of his growing political maturity and an advance on his position of *Labour in Irish History*. They argue that he espoused the notion that an alliance with the national bourgeoisie was now essential for Irish freedom. But nowhere does he abandon the belief that the working class was the sole inheritor of the fight for Irish freedom, nor does he ever adopt the stages theory and accept that the outcome of the uprising would be a bourgeois capitalist republic. It is more likely that the aftermath of working class defeats drove Connolly into a closer accommodation to Republican politics than he would have liked. Indeed in *Erin's Hope* as early as 1897 Connolly had written, 'No revolutionist can safely invite the cooperation of men or classes whose ideals are not theirs and whom, therefore, they may be compelled to fight at some future critical stage of the journey to freedom.'

Berresford-Ellis argues that this view was later revised in favour of Lenin's formulation quoted above, but as I have already argued this sleight of hand is an attempt to justify both his and Greaves' view that the Irish revolution would have to come in stages.

So what of Connolly's legacy? Every shade of political opinion in Ireland has tried to claim him as one of their own. His revolutionary politics have invariably been watered down or conveniently forgotten. He is remembered for his leading role in the 1916 uprising, the final act of his life, and not for all that went before it. His irrevocable commitment to working class struggle, his internationalism and his implacable hostility to reformism are all conveniently sidelined. Part of the reason for this is that he did not bequeath a political organisation that could carry through his political vision in the years after his death. Those who fought alongside him in the unions accepted de Valera's dictum that the aspirations of workers had to be subordinated to the development of an independent Irish state even to the extent of supporting Fianna Fail, an openly capitalist party. Indeed, the Irish Citizen's Army dissolved itself into the Dublin brigade of the IRA led by Oscar Traynor, an ally of de Valera. Those who fought alongside him for national liberation accepted something less than freedom in the wake of Ireland's partition in 1921 in the Treaty which established the Southern Irish state.

It wasn't as if Connolly had no desire to build a socialist organisation that could survive his death. All his life he had been involved in creating or seeking to sustain socialist parties, but his understanding of their role was flawed. His period in the US had seen him influenced by the syndicalist tradition which elevated the importance of militant trade unionism above the need for building an independent political party. Connolly regarded political struggles as an echo of industrial struggles and not as something that required their own specific organisational form.

The defeat of the Dublin workers in 1913 brought into sharper relief Connolly's view that militant Republicans would automatically be drawn to socialist politics during the course of the struggle for national liberation. However, the lack of an independent political voice meant that the class interests of workers were subordinated to the class interests of the national bourgeoisie in the emerging Southern Irish state. The partition of Ireland and the creation of the Northern state divided workers along religious lines and led to decades of discrimination and oppression against the Catholic minority. Connolly's vision of a united movement of Catholic and Protestant workers, North and South of the border did not have the organisational vehicle to become a reality.

This article has focused on the debate arising out of the introductions to these collections, but it is illuminating to highlight some of the examples that make Connolly's writings so compelling. In *Labour, Religion and Nationality* he engages in debate with the Jesuit priest Father Kane who used the pulpit to denounce the increasing levels of organisation and political consciousness among the Dublin workers. In his Lenten discourses in 1910 he denounced socialism for leading to the rule of the mob. Connolly's response undermines the impact of the 'insult' by taking it as a compliment and throwing it back in the face of the cleric. In one of his most powerful passages he gives voice to the role of the masses in history:

> There was a time stretching for more than 1,000 years, when the mob was without power or influence, when the entire power of the world was concentrated in the hands of the kings, the nobles and the hierarchy. That was the blackest period in human history... Then the mob started on its upward march to power—a power only to be realised in the socialist republic. In the course of its upward march the mob has transformed and humanised the world. It has abolished religious persecution and imposed toleration on bigots of all creeds; it has established the value of human life; softened the horrors of war as a preliminary to abolishing it; compelled trial by jury; abolished the death penalty...and today is fighting to take children from the factory and the mine and put them in school...in this civilising, humanising work the mob had at all times to meet and master the hatred of kings and nobles and there is not in history a record of any movement for abolishing torture, preventing war, establishing popular suffrage, or shortening the hours of labour led by the hierarchy... All hail to the mob, the incarnation of progress![14]

Echoing Marx on the self-emancipation of the working class, he celebrates the self-activity of the masses in transforming the world in the face of undying opposition from the ruling elites. Writing in *The Workers' Republic* he ridicules Keir Hardie's attempts to portray the Irish Home Rule Party as progressive by illustrating how it had opposed every single attempt by Hardie himself to draw attention in parliament to the plight of workers. If it was so profoundly reactionary in the House of Commons, how could its strategy for Ireland be any different?

Connolly's writings have an astonishing breadth of reference. Some, like his attacks on Celtic mysticism and pan-Nationalist alliances, have a clear resonance for today's struggle. He accuses the Celtic myth makers of an 'unprogressive desire to escape the responsibility of investigating phenomena by placing their source beyond the reach of human activity'. Others have a more internationalist flavour whether celebrating the anti-war stance of the Russian socialists or discussing the general prospects for revolution in Europe. In an article on the struggle in Germany written at the start of the war in 1914 he writes, 'To me, therefore, the socialist of another country is a fellow patriot, as the capitalist of my own country is a natural enemy.' In a biting assessment of the British Social Democratic Federation he concludes that 'there was a revolutionary activity and fight once in the SDF, but their leaders, Hyndman, Quelch and Burrows, have led it as a lightning conductor leads lightning—into the earth to dissipate its energy.'

For these and countless other sharply written insights, Connolly's own writings repay their readers and arm them with arguments for the struggle. For making a selection of his work accessible both these collections are welcome. But neither pay Connolly the respect due to his thoroughgoing commitment to revolution by providing a critical assessment of his life and work. For that Allen's political biography is indispensable.

Notes

1   'Labour and the Proposed Partition of Ireland', *Irish Worker*, 14 March 1914.
2   Ibid.
3   Quoted in E Mallie and D McKitterick, *The Fight for Peace* (Heinemann, 1996).
4   A Morgan, *James Connolly: a Political Biography* (Manchester University Press, 1988).
5   C D Greaves, *The Life and Times of James Connolly* (Lawrence & Wishart, 1988).
6   P Berresford-Ellis, *A History of the Irish Working Class* (Pluto, 1985).
7   *Irish Worker*, 29 August 1914.
8   J Connolly, *Labour in Irish History* (Bookmarks 1987).
9   Quoted in P Berresford-Ellis, *Selected Writings: James Connolly* (Pluto, 1997), pix.
10 Quoted in K Allen, op cit, p170.
11 C D Greaves, op cit, p36.
12 Quoted ibid, p37.
13 See T Cliff, *Lenin* vol 2 (Pluto, 1975), p127.
14 P Berresford-Ellis, op cit, p8.

The Socialist Workers Party is one of an international grouping of socialist organisations:

AUSTRALIA:	International Socialists, PO Box A338, Sydney South
BELGIUM	Socialisme International, 80, Rue Bois Gotha, 4000 Liége
BRITAIN:	Socialist Workers Party, PO Box 82, London E3
CANADA:	International Socialists, PO Box 339, Station E, Toronto, Ontario M6H 4E3
CYPRUS:	Ergatiki Demokratia, PO Box 7280, Nicosia
DENMARK:	Internationale Socialister, Postboks 642, 2200 København N
GERMANY:	Linksruck, Postfach 304 183, 20359 Hamburg
GREECE:	Sosialistiko Ergatiko Komma, c/o Workers Solidarity, PO Box 8161, Athens 100 10
HOLLAND:	Internationale Socialisten, PO Box 92052, 1090 AA Amsterdam
IRELAND:	Socialist Workers Party, PO Box 1648, Dublin 8
NEW ZEALAND:	Socialist Workers Organization, PO Box 8851, Auckland
NORWAY:	Internasjonale Socialisterr, Postboks 9226 Grønland, 0134 Oslo
POLAND:	Solidarność Socjalistyczna, PO Box 12, 01-900 Warszawa 118
SOUTH AFRICA:	Socialist Workers Organisation, PO Box 18530, Hillbrow 2038, Johannesberg
SPAIN:	Socialismo Internacional, Apartado 563, 08080, Barcelona
UNITED STATES:	International Socialist Organisation, PO Box 16085, Chicago, Illinois 60616
ZIMBABWE:	International Socialist Organisation, PO Box 6758, Harare

The following issues of *International Socialism* (second series) are available price £3 (including postage) from IS Journal, PO Box 82, London E3 3LH. *International Socialism* 2:58 and 2:65 are available on cassette from the Royal National Institute for the Blind (Peterborough Library Unit). Phone 01733 370777.

International Socialism 2:79 Summer 1998
John Rees: The return of Marx? ★ Lindsey German: Reflections on *The Communist Manifesto* ★ Judy Cox: An introduction to Marx's theory of alienation ★ Judith Orr: Making a comeback: the Marxist theory of crisis ★ Megan Trudell: New Labour, old conflicts: the story so far ★ John Molyneux: State of the art ★ Anna Chen: In perspective: Sergei Eisenstein ★ Jonathan Neale: Vietnam Veterans ★ Phil Gasper: Bookwatch: Marxism and science ★

International Socialism 2:78 Spring 1998
Colin Sparks: The eye of the storm ★ Shin Gyoung-hee: The crisis and the workers' movement in South Korea ★ Rob Hoveman: Financial crises and the real economy ★ Peter Morgan: Class divisions in the gay community ★ Alex Callinicos: The secret of the dialectic ★ John Parrington: It's life, Jim, but not as we know it ★ Judy Cox: Robin Hood: earl, outlaw or rebel? ★ Ian Birchall: The vice-like hold of nationalism? A comment on Megan Trudell's 'Prelude to revolution' ★ William Keach: In perspective: Alexander Cockburn and Christopher Hitchens ★

International Socialism 2:77 Winter 1997
Audrey Farrell: Addicted to profit—capitalism and drugs ★ Mike Gonzalez: The resurrections of Che Guevara ★ Sam Ashman: India: imperialism, partition and resistance ★ Henry Maitles: Never Again! ★ John Baxter: The return of political science ★ Dave Renton: Past its peak ★

International Socialism 2:76 Autumn 1997
Mike Haynes: Was there a parliamentary alternative in 1917? ★ Megan Trudell: Prelude to revolution: class consciousness and the First World War ★ Judy Cox: A light in the darkness ★ Pete Glatter: Victor Serge: writing for the future ★ Gill Hubbard: A guide to action ★ Chris Bambery: Review article: Labour's history of hope and despair ★

International Socialism 2:75 Summer 1997
John Rees: The class struggle under New Labour ★ Alex Callinicos: Europe: the mounting crisis ★ Lance Selfa: Mexico after the Zapatista uprising ★ William Keach: Rise like lions? Shelley and the revolutionary left ★ Judy Cox: What state are we really in? ★ John Parrington: In perspective: Valentin Voloshinov ★

International Socialism 2:74 Spring 1997
Colin Sparks: Tories, Labour and the crisis in education ★ Colin Wilson: The politics of information technology ★ Mike Gonzalez: No more heroes: Nicaragua 1996 ★ Christopher Hill: Tulmults and commotions: turning the world upside down ★ Peter Morgan: Capitalism without frontiers? ★ Alex Callinicos: Minds, machines and evolution ★ Anthony Arnove: In perspective: Noam Chomsky★

International Socialism 2:73 Winter 1996
Chris Harman: Globalisation: a critique of a new orthodoxy ★ Chris Bambery: Marxism and sport ★ John Parrington: Computers and consciousness: a reply to Alex Callinicos ★ Joe Faith: Dennett, materialism and empiricism ★ Megan Trudell: Who made the American Revolution? ★ Mark O'Brien: The class conflicts which shaped British history ★ John Newsinger: From class war to Cold War ★ Alex Callinicos: The state in debate ★ Charlie Kimber: Review article: coming to terms with barbarism in Rwanda in Burundi★

International Socialism 2:72 Autumn 1996
Alex Callinicos: Betrayal and discontent: Labour under Blair ★ Sue Cockerill and Colin Sparks: Japan in crisis ★ Richard Levins: When science fails us ★ Ian Birchall: The Babeuf bicentenary: conspiracy or revolutionary party? ★ Brian Manning: A voice for the poor ★ Paul O'Flinn: From the kingdom of necessity to the kingdom of freedom: Morris's *News from Nowhere* ★ Clare Fermont: Bookwatch: Palestine and the Middle East 'peace process'★

International Socialism 2:71 Summer 1996
Chris Harman: The crisis of bourgeois economics ★ Hassan Mahamdallie: William Morris and revolutionary Marxism ★ Alex Callinicos: Darwin, materialism and revolution ★ Chris Nineham: Raymond Williams: revitalising the left? ★ Paul Foot: A passionate prophet of liberation ★ Gill Hubbard: Why has feminism failed women? ★ Lee Sustar: Bookwatch: fighting to unite black and white★

International Socialism 2:70 Spring 1996
Alex Callinicos: South Africa after apartheid ★ Chris Harman: France's hot December ★ Brian Richardson: The making of a revolutionary ★ Gareth Jenkins: Why Lucky Jim turned right—an obituary of Kingsley Amis ★ Mark O'Brien: The bloody birth of capitalism ★ Lee Humber: Studies in revolution ★ Adrian Budd: A new life for Lenin ★ Martin Smith: Bookwatch: the General Strike★

International Socialism 2:69 Winter 1995
Lindsey German: The Balkan war: can there be peace? ★ Duncan Blackie: The left and the Balkan war ★ Nicolai Gentchev: The myth of welfare dependency ★ Judy Cox: Wealth, poverty and class in Britain today ★ Peter Morgan: Trade unions and strikes ★ Julie Waterson: The party at its peak ★ Megan Trudell: Living to some purpose ★ Nick Howard: The rise and fall of socialism in one city ★ Andy Durgan: Bookwatch: Civil war and revolution in Spain ★

International Socialism 2:68 Autumn 1995
Ruth Brown: Racism and immigration in Britain ★ John Molyneux: Is Marxism deterministic? ★ Stuart Hood: News from nowhere? ★ Lee Sustar: Communism in the heart of the beast ★ Peter Linebaugh: To the teeth and forehead of our faults ★ George Paizis: Back to the future ★ Phil Marshall: The children of stalinism ★ Paul D'Amato: Bookwatch: 100 years of cinema ★

International Socialism 2:67 Summer 1995
Paul Foot: When will the Blair bubble burst? ★ Chris Harman: From Bernstein to Blair—100 years of revisionism ★ Chris Bambery: Was the Second World War a war for democracy? ★ Alex Callinicos: Hope against the Holocaust ★Chris Nineham: Is the media all powerful? ★ Peter Morgan: How the West was won ★ Charlie Hore: Bookwatch: China since Mao ★

International Socialism 2:66 Spring 1995
Dave Crouch: The crisis in Russia and the rise of the right ★ Phil Gasper: Cruel and unusual punishment: the politics of crime in the United States ★ Alex Callinicos: Backwards to liberalism ★ John Newsinger: Matewan: film and working class struggle ★ John Rees: The light and the dark ★ Judy Cox: How to make the Tories disappear ★ Charlie Hore: Jazz: a reply to the critics ★ Pat Riordan: Bookwatch: Ireland ★

International Socialism 2:65 Special issue
Lindsey German: Frederick Engels: life of a revolutionary ★ John Rees: Engels' Marxism ★ Chris Harman: Engels and the origins of human society ★ Paul McGarr: Engels and natural science ★

International Socialism 2:64 Autumn 1994
Chris Harman: The prophet and the proletariat ★ Kieran Allen: What is changing in Ireland ★ Mike Haynes: The wrong road on Russia ★ Rob Ferguson: Hero and villain ★ Jane Elderton: Suffragette style ★ Chris Nineham: Two faces of modernism ★ Mike Hobart, Dave Harker and Matt Kelly: Three replies to 'Jazz—a people's music?' ★ Charlie Kimber: Bookwatch: South Africa—the struggle continues ★

International Socialism 2:63 Summer 1994
Alex Callinicos: Crisis and class struggle in Europe today ★ Duncan Blackie: The United Nations and the politics of imperialism ★ Brian Manning: The English Revolution and the transition from feudalism to capitalism ★ Lee Sustar: The roots of multi-racial labour unity in the United States ★ Peter Linebaugh: Days of villainy: a reply to two critics ★ Dave Sherry: Trotsky's last, greatest struggle ★ Peter Morgan: Geronimo and the end of the Indian wars ★ Dave Beecham: Ignazio Silone and *Fontamara* ★ Chris Bambery: Bookwatch: understanding fascism ★

International Socialism 2:62 Spring 1994
Sharon Smith: Mistaken identity—or can identity politics liberate the oppressed? ★ Iain Ferguson: Containing the crisis—crime and the Tories ★ John Newsinger: Orwell and the Spanish Revolution ★ Chris Harman: Change at the first millenium ★ Adrian Budd: Nation and empire—Labour's foreign policy 1945-51 ★ Gareth Jenkins: Novel questions ★ Judy Cox: Blake's revolution ★ Derek Howl: Bookwatch: the Russian Revolution ★

International Socialism 2:61 Winter 1994
Lindsey German: Before the flood? ★ John Molyneux: The 'politically correct' controversy ★ David McNally: E P Thompson—class struggle and historical materialism ★ Charlie Hore: Jazz—a people's music ★ Donny Gluckstein: Revolution and the challenge of labour ★ Charlie Kimber: Bookwatch: the Labour Party in decline ★

International Socialism 2:59 Summer 1993
Ann Rogers: Back to the workhouse ★ Kevin Corr and Andy Brown: The labour aristocracy and the roots of reformism ★ Brian Manning: God, Hill and Marx ★ Henry Maitles: Cutting the wire: a criticial appraisal of Primo Levi ★ Hazel Croft: Bookwatch: women and work ★

International Socialism 2:58 Spring 1993
Chris Harman: Where is capitalism going? (part one) ★ Ruth Brown and Peter Morgan: Politics and the class struggle today: a roundtable discussion ★ Richard Greeman: The return of Comrade Tulayev: Victor Serge and the tragic vision of Stalinism ★ Norah Carlin: A new English revolution ★ John Charlton: Building a new world ★ Colin Barker: A reply to Dave McNally ★

International Socialism 2:56 Autumn 1992
Chris Harman: The Return of the National Question ★ Dave Treece: Why the Earth Summit failed ★ Mike Gonzalez: Can Castro survive? ★ Lee Humber and John Rees: The good old cause—an interview with Christopher Hill ★ Ernest Mandel: The Impasse of Schematic Dogmatism ★

International Socialism 2:55 Summer 1992
Alex Callinicos: Race and class ★ Lee Sustar: Racism and class struggle in the American Civil War era ★ Lindsey German and Peter Morgan: Prospects for socialists—an interview with Tony Cliff ★ Robert Service: Did Lenin lead to Stalin? ★ Samuel Farber: In defence of democratic revolutionary socialism ★ David Finkel: Defending 'October' or sectarian dogmatism? ★ Robin Blackburn: Reply to John Rees ★ John Rees: Dedicated followers of fashion ★ Colin Barker: In praise of custom ★ Sheila McGregor: Revolutionary witness ★

International Socialism 2:54 Spring 1992
Sharon Smith: Twilight of the American dream ★ Mike Haynes: Class and crisis—the transition in eastern Europe ★ Costas Kossis: A miracle without end? Japanese capitalism and the world economy ★ Alex Callinicos: Capitalism and the state system: A reply to Nigel Harris ★ Steven Rose: Do animals have rights? ★ John Charlton: Crime and class in the 18th century ★ John Rees: Revolution, reform and working class culture ★ Chris Harman: Blood simple ★

International Socialism 2:51 Summer 1991
Chris Harman: The state and capitalism today ★ Alex Callinicos: The end of nationalism? ★ Sharon Smith: Feminists for a strong state? ★ Colin Sparks and Sue Cockerill: Goodbye to the Swedish miracle ★ Simon Phillips: The South African Communist Party and the South African working class ★ John Brown: Class conflict and the crisis of feudalism ★

International Socialism 2:49 Winter 1990
Chris Bambery: The decline of the Western Communist Parties ★ Ernest Mandel: A theory which has not withstood the test of time ★ Chris Harman: Criticism which does not withstand the test of logic ★ Derek Howl: The law of value In the USSR ★ Terry Eagleton: Shakespeare and the class struggle ★ Lionel Sims: Rape and pre-state societies ★ Sheila McGregor: A reply to Lionel Sims ★

International Socialism 2:48 Autumn 1990
Lindsey German: The last days of Thatcher ★ John Rees: The new imperialism ★ Neil Davidson and Donny Gluckstein: Nationalism and the class struggle in Scotland ★ Paul McGarr: Order out of chaos ★

International Socialism 2:46 Winter 1989
Chris Harman: The storm breaks ★ Alex Callinicos: Can South Africa be reformed? ★ John Saville: Britain, the Marshall Plan and the Cold War ★ Sue Clegg: Against the stream ★ John Rees: The rising bourgeoisie ★

International Socialism 2:44 Autumn 1989
Charlie Hore: China: Tiananmen Square and after ★ Sue Clegg: Thatcher and the welfare state ★ John Molyneux: *Animal Farm* revisited ★ David Finkel: After Arias, is the revolution over? ★ John Rose: Jews in Poland ★

International Socialism 2:41 Winter 1988
Polish socialists speak out: Solidarity at the Crossroads ★ Mike Haynes: Nightmares of the market ★ Jack Robertson: Socialists and the unions ★ Andy Strouthous: Are the unions in decline? ★ Richard Bradbury: What is Post-Structuralism? ★ Colin Sparks: George Bernard Shaw ★

International Socialism 2:39 Summer 1988
Chris Harman and Andy Zebrowski: Glasnost, before the storm ★ Chanie Rosenberg: Labour and the fight against fascism ★ Mike Gonzalez: Central America after the Peace Plan ★ Ian Birchall: Raymond Williams ★ Alex Callinicos: Reply to John Rees ★

International Socialism 2:35 Summer 1987
Pete Green: Capitalism and the Thatcher years ★ Alex Callinicos: Imperialism, capitalism and the state today ★ Ian Birchall: Five years of *New Socialist* ★ Callinicos and Wood debate 'Looking for alternatives to reformism' ★ David Widgery replies on 'Beating Time' ★

International Socialism 2:30 Autumn 1985
Gareth Jenkins: Where is the Labour Party heading? ★ David McNally: Debt, inflation and the rate of profit ★ Ian Birchall: The terminal crisis in the British Communist Party ★ replies on Women's oppression and *Marxism Today* ★

International Socialism 2:29 Summer 1985
Special issue on the class struggle and the left in the aftermath of the miners' defeat ★ Tony Cliff: Patterns of mass strike ★ Chris Harman: 1984 and the shape of things to come ★ Alex Callinicos: The politics of *Marxism Today* ★

International Socialism 2:26 Spring 1985
Pete Green: Contradictions of the American boom ★ Colin Sparks: Labour and imperialism ★ Chris Bambery: Marx and Engels and the unions ★ Sue Cockerill: The municipal road to socialism ★ Norah Carlin: Is the family part of the superstructure? ★ Kieran Allen: James Connolly and the 1916 rebellion ★

International Socialism 2:25 Autumn 1984
John Newsinger: Jim Larkin, Syndicalism and the 1913 Dublin Lockout ★ Pete Binns: Revolution and state capitalism in the Third World ★ Colin Sparks: Towards a police state? ★ Dave Lyddon: Demystifying the downturn ★ John Molyneux: Do working class men benefit from women's oppression? ★

International Socialism 2:18 Winter 1983
Donny Gluckstein: Workers' councils in Western Europe ★ Jane Ure Smith: The early Communist press in Britain ★ John Newsinger: The Bolivian Revolution ★ Andy Durgan: Largo Caballero and Spanish socialism ★ M Barker and A Beezer: Scarman and the language of racism ★

International Socialism 2:14 Winter 1981
Chris Harman: The riots of 1981 ★ Dave Beecham: Class struggle under the Tories ★ Tony Cliff: Alexandra Kollontai ★ L James and A Paczuska: Socialism needs feminism ★ reply to Cliff on Zetkin ★ Feminists In the labour movement ★

International Socialism 2:13 Summer 1981
Chris Harman: The crisis last time ★ Tony Cliff: Clara Zetkin ★ Ian Birchall: Left Social Democracy In the French Popular Front ★ Pete Green: Alternative Economic Strategy ★ Tim Potter: The death of Eurocommunism ★